His Quiet Splendor

BILL STARR
CHAR MEREDITH

*His
Quiet
Splendor*

Reflections on God's Love

WORD BOOKS
PUBLISHER
4800 WEST WACO DRIVE
WACO, TEXAS
76703

Illustrations by O. Stanley Miller

Grateful acknowledgment is made for permission to use on page 88
the excerpt from *Notes on Love and Courage* by Hugh Prather.
Copyright © 1977 by Hugh Prather. Reprinted by permission of
Doubleday & Company, Inc.

Scripture quotations identified PHILLIPS are from *The New Testament
in Modern English,* copyright © 1958, 1960, 1972 by J. B. Phillips
and reprinted with permission of Macmillan Publishing Co., Inc.
Quotations marked TLB are from *The Living Bible, Paraphrased*
(Wheaton: Tyndale House Publishers, © 1971), used by permission.
Quotations marked AMPLIFIED are from *The Amplified New Testament,*
© The Lockman Foundation 1958, and used by permission.
Quotations marked KJV are from the King James Version of
the Bible.

ISBN 0-8499-0129-4
Library of Congress catalog card number: 81-52526
Printed in the United States of America

Contents

6 CONTENTS

A Note from the Authors

This is a book about love. Funny we didn't recognize that when we started writing it. We began with some exhilarating thoughts about Creation, and about Incarnation. At one point we were talking about Miracles. At another, we mused about Revelation—and the various ways God shows us who He is. But now that it is written it becomes very evident that what we were considering all along is love. It was so simple we had to laugh at our own tedious process.

Quickly we cycled back to what we both consider the Source—God, and the Biblical tenet that God is love; and we saw that back at the beginning of everything, way back before the worlds were formed, love had to be present. Before anything else was, there was love—waiting, needing, persisting, clamoring to be expressed in some perceivable form. Just as it is today.

What forms does God use to express that love? We have concentrated our reflections here on three very basic ones: Creation, Incarnation, and Human Relationship. What we have come out with is in no way an exhaustive thesis or a theological position paper. We think we have

brought together a few common little human stories that
any inquiring person can respond to. This is not a book
that is going to require detailed study; we do hope it will
take you beyond where you already are. For those who
want to struggle there are scenes included that probably
will require a fight to go deeper on an individual search,
and the conclusions may come out at a place that is
different from ours.

Actually, this is a series of conversations—explorations
and discoveries—between friends. Each time we got
together there was a high point, a "We-e-ell, Charlotte!"
or a "You've got it, Bill!"—"Aha's" that cried out to be
shared.

What we hope is that you will pull up a chair and join
us as you can. Each chapter seeks to capture one
conversation, and is complete in itself. You don't have to
read the whole book before you dampen down the fire in
the grate, or turn off the light. There is a thread that
emerges throughout the chapters, however, and we see
that as LOVE.

So here it is. It's scary to put it out before you. We know
you won't like all of it; we know some of you could have
done a far more scholarly job; but it was a task given to
us and we offer these pages to you with a sense of
expectancy. It's been an exciting process, an overwhelming
one at times. We have been awed and angered, amused
and boggled. Our hope is that the process will go on in
you as you read, and that the Spirit of God will bring you
gently to your own amazements.

I. *God Reveals His Love in Creation*

1. *In the Mountains*

High in the Rocky Mountains, we were making our way through a meadow of wild flowers that reached up to our knees. There was no way we could take a step and not crush them. I had been climbing steadily for an hour with two hundred high school campers. The snow field, our destination, seemed stitched like a giant cotton patch to the green slope above and beyond us. The sound of melted snow trickling in the stream bed mixed with the wind strumming the pines. I stepped up alongside a girl who had stopped to absorb the spectacular panorama of sky and rugged peaks.

Without looking at me she breathed, "You guys have got it rigged." I knew what she was feeling. "There's no way we can come up here and see all this and not believe in God!"

I remember laughing out loud. She was so correct. I think her exclamation gave God pleasure, too. After all, I mused, it proved His point!

So many times when we take kids up in the mountains, they stand there and just want to drink it in. It's so vast.

It's so breathtaking. It gives them a feeling that "He is something else! He must really be huge!" Higher up, above timberline, we walk along and point out those intricate little blue forget-me-nots, a marmot scurrying from hole to hole, the brilliant scraps of carpet on the rocks. Suddenly they realize that that BIG God does those tiny little things also, and they get a tough, but oh so gentle sense of God, and it flips them. He's big and huge, but He's warm and thoughtful. Who would think to put a little flower here? What are the chances of anyone seeing it? What fun He must have hiding a surprise way up here for the few people who'll notice—people who are dog-tired, who can't even look up, but who as they're looking down discover a beautiful flower in miniature. How God must enjoy letting people have that pleasure! Doesn't that indicate a lot about Him?

Sometimes the shifting of the wind up there brings utter quietness. I don't think many high school boys and girls have ever heard silence; always in their lives there is noise; it's just a matter of how much. But high on that mountain, when everyone is standing still, and the wind has stopped, the silence is thunderous.

To talk with kids after we come down is the real fun, to watch their expressions as we reiterate the thrill of standing on the top of a mountain, of looking out over the valley below to see the world that goes out and out and out beyond us. The immensity of the mountain, and the feeling of one's own tininess makes it not hard for them to comprehend: "Boy! there's got to be Somebody. And He must be BIG, BIG, BIG!" Then the realization comes, "He must be big enough to take care of my problems. Hey! He's big enough to handle my girlfriend."

From the very beginning it appears that God has been desiring to make Himself known to us. How awesome it is to be exposed to the marvels of His creation—full force! How much we need that time that puts us in touch with the works of His hands.

We get so used to the distractions that hinder us from delighting in the glory of God around us that we scarcely recognize them as distractions. Sounds and images bombard our waking hours. Thoughts, assignments, and requests tyrannize our days. Attention to details squeezes us to see with a sort of tunnel vision. All these demands blot out so much of the sheer joy of aliveness that we often miss the central thrust of life itself. . . .

It was so healthy for me to get out on the mountain again! The shape of the mountain peaks always overwhelms me—even though we (my family and I) woke to their clearly etched lines every morning for more than a dozen years. The metal treasure buried inside those ranges is a compelling mystery. The limitless wash of waves along the shore has a similar effect, and the food resources contained in the deep seas. The comical design of a hippopotamus or a giraffe—the exquisite detail of a hummingbird or a butterfly—God is saying something about Himself in every finished piece.

So many of us run over the natural wonders about us so quickly, yet there seems no excuse for us not to know Him if we are really looking for Him. I believe He expected us to know Him through the works of His hands, that His expression to us in Creation is an infinite effort to reveal Himself to us in love.

That's why He did it all—*for us*. The diversity, the uniqueness, the differences in animal life and people life; the colors and fragrances, patterns and textures—all are a kaleidoscopic expression of His love. That's what revelation is—the revealing of oneself—*that is loving!* To unfold, to open up, to express—all of that is loving. Revealing and loving are really part and parcel of the same thing. That's a link I've missed most of my life—the idea of loving someone enough to *work at* revealing who I am, as God did in Creation.

As we hikers walked on under the vast dome of Colorado sky, I thought about the first two pages of the book of Genesis. Here must be the most concise description in all of literature, concerning the most monumental of all happenings: God began to create the universe out of a formless desolation engulfed in total darkness. The power of God began to move, and in the space of two brief chapters all things had come into being! Day, night, sky, earth, seas, plants, seasons, sunshine, moon, stars, birds, animals. And finally, in an ultimate triumphant act above and beyond all the other marvels, the first human was formed; a suitable companion for him was added; and together they became the managers over all the rest of His creation—the earth and all its resources!

This compact record of the Creation suddenly spotlights for me three core relationships: (1) between man and his God, (2) between man and his environment, and (3) between husband and wife. All of this expressed through Creation begins to tell me something. Creation is more than a scientific wonder! It contains strong personal implications for all of us twentieth-century humans.

It looks to me as if this kind of revealing love—the kind that doesn't count any cost too great—is the transforming element in life. Loving is what makes life worth living. It's the fulfillment area, the essence. Without it, where is life?

2. *In Nature*

We were looking out from the sixth floor onto a patch of winter wilderness between two expressways. A couple of pheasants, as though on cue, slid to a landing in the brown weeds, and then took off anew. In the rush of man-made traffic, God was there again, revealing Himself in a flurry of beauty and grace. But how to think of Him *before* the pheasants were created? *Before* the falling snow? *Before* the earth and the weeds? How can we think of Him apart from anything that was made? Is it possible for us humans to know love unless it is expressed in a tangible form? We struggle to push our minds back to the beginning where God existed before any of His acts of creation.

We're told that in the beginning there was God. We believe that God is love, and because He is love He has to do something to express that love. Maybe He starts with this "void," doing something with it. Maybe He's rolling it around in His hands as a piece of clay is molded. Maybe He's weaving strands of it together, or carving it into a new shape. Whatever He does to express His love, a couple of things seem necessary: first, it must be something that accurately reveals who He is; and, second,

this revealing process must generate a response in us, His creatures.

Bringing these thoughts down to someone we know who is creating something may help. An artist. A sculptor. A wood carver. A musician. For example, a young artist whose work I follow with extreme interest and respect has an intense need through her art to "make a statement" that is significant. Whether her expression comes out in the form of a commercial cartoon, a fine painting, a wood cut, or a clay figure, it will reveal something of who she is. And no matter how reluctant she may be to show it to me, the fact remains that it will call forth a response in me. The response she arouses is not always the kind she would wish for; but she *has* to risk that possible rejection of her work because her need to get it out where it can be responded to is so strong.

In the New Testament Paul says,

> It is not that they do not know the truth about God: indeed he has made it quite plain to them. For since the beginning of the world the invisible attributes of God, e.g. His eternal power and divinity have been plainly discernible through things which He has made and which are commonly seen and known, thus leaving these men without a rag of an excuse. They knew all the time that there is a God, yet they refused to acknowledge him as such, or to thank him for what he is or does (Rom. 1:19-21, Phillips).

Isn't that a pistol of a passage? Paul figures "*they are without excuse*" because they can see so much of Him just by looking at what He has made. It boggles my mind to think I might accurately grasp the attributes of Almighty God simply through my experience of Nature. We are so far removed in our sophisticated society from Nature's existing by itself that we tend to balk at the idea of an unlettered nomad finding salvation.

Consider a mother or father in a remote rain forest, perhaps a primitive tribesman—someone we don't even know exists. All his life he has been surrounded by Creation. Wouldn't you like to know what he infers about God's eternal power and divinity from the environment around him? What do the tall fruit-heavy banana plants or the huge tree he shapes into a dugout canoe tell him?

What say the early morning mists that rise from the river, the fiery orange moon emerging from the lake, making a path of light across the water, and turning to cold white as it lifts in the sky? What about the frogs and lizards and funny peanut bugs and the large shiny beetles? The vines as fat as an arm, the breadfruit tree with its spiny green balls, the emerald moss dripping with rain, the extravaganza of plants, clusters of papayas and the ambrosia-sweet mangoes, the bushes drooping with berries, seeds, and nuts? What about the whole world of fish, and the brilliant assortment of birds and flowers? Even more difficult, what does he infer from the stinging nettles, the briars, the black furry-legged tarantulas, the snakes, the flood of mud and water that drowns his village site?

Such remote, unsophisticated tribespeople have had no words, no books, no outside contact, no verbal messages to teach them about the origin and purpose of life. Yet, there is something in that plethora of life, those natural elemental happenings, that powerfully draws them toward the Giver. Some respond with grateful hearts and a simple "Yes, Lord," while others choose to refuse to respond.

> They knew all the time that there is a God, yet they refused to acknowledge him as such, or to thank him for what he is or does. . . . They gave up God: and therefore God gave them up . . . (Rom. 1:21, 24, Phillips).

In the Philippines I met a man who is a leader in the affairs of a distant province. During lunch he spoke about the "faith" of his people, especially those in the rural areas. "*Blind* faith," he called it. I tried to tap into that. He explained about the powerful effects of Nature—the thunder, the lightning, the rains that fall on the fields, things that grow, the food provided by the warm climate. All of these, he told me, give rise to an innate sense of Someone who is providing. There is no doubt in their minds that there is a God who is caring for them through His provision in Nature.

Another Filipino leader, who has lived a lōng and useful life, volunteered, "I derive my daily strength from the deep conviction that there is a Power who guides our destinies, and who oversees everything that is taking place everyday." I could sense the worship in him as he continued, "I cannot believe that man was made by accident. I cannot believe that the universe came through happenstance. There must have been a Grand Designer."

Granted, these influential men are not without verbal input—from their church, the university, the holy Scriptures, their friends and associates, printed materials. Still, they do speak from a perspective much closer to the realm of Nature than most Westerners can. Something comes through Creation that indicates to their people a superior Being, a Force, a spiritual environment that is close and real. Perhaps it comes through more clearly to people who are immersed in God's Creation. A surplus of human invention and production tends to grab our attention; we're prone to layer our lives and our desires with all that man has done rather than with the evidences of what God is doing.

Millions of people over the centuries, since the first man and woman, have had no verbal input about a Father in Heaven, or about His Son Jesus. There's *got* to be some way for them to get to know their Maker. There must be some way in which the broad sweep of Creation speaks to them. The nonverbal has to be very significant in God's plan. We must allow ourselves to believe that something of His *love,* His care, His provision comes through the wonders of His world.

" . . . not that we loved God, but that God loved us . . ."
(1 John 4:10)

3. *Creation Is for Us*

Over the years in Colorado I watched the manager of
Young Life's Frontier Ranch. Bill Mitchell would wait
ever so patiently by a chipmunk hole, sometimes for an
hour. Eventually a little animal would come out and Bill
would grab it. He had a way of taming these creatures,
just petting them on the back of the neck, stroking and
stroking, until they would nod off to sleep, sort of
hypnotized. Bill would put the chipmunk into his shirt
pocket and let it sleep as he went about his work. When it
started to wiggle, he would take it out, pet it again, play
with it and give it something to eat. Pretty soon the little
wild thing would be tame. Big kids from the heart of New
York City would watch him, entranced. Then they would
look for a chipmunk of their own to tame. They would
keep it in a shirt pocket, walk around camp with it riding
on a shoulder; and before they left the wildness of the
Rockies they would build little crates and carry those soft
furry creatures back to the tough old city.

The effect of that expression of the wild becoming tame
enough to touch, to handle, to claim, intrigues me. Even
though we sometimes do these fascinating creatures more
harm than good, the power of Nature over us says

something to me—the softness of the animal's skin, or perhaps the hardness. We see all the paradoxes: the gentle sensitive doe and the rough rumbly bear; the skittish cat and the slithery snake. So many clues we can follow: the wind which can be so warm and sensual and soft, can also be biting and cruel and destructive. Creation holds many great paradoxical secrets. Paul says it is enough for faith, and that the reason for Creation is that we may *know God.*

Another reason for Creation is that *man is to master it.* God asks man to name everything He has made. He puts the man and his wife into His freshly minted earth, and assigns them to take care of it. They are to get control over this new world, to manage its resources, to keep it all going. This gives men and women a worthwhile activity for the years of their lives. God has built into Creation all kinds of secrets to be discovered, to keep us curious and busy, not only for the extent of our own lifetime but for eons. We are designed so that we will struggle with this old planet, explore it, research its resources—trying to find answers to our questions, solutions to our needs and desires.

It is fulfilling for man, with the intellect God gave him, to find out, for instance, about petroleum under the surface of the earth or to find gases that are useful. It absorbs a person's life to puzzle over the force that tugs pairs of objects toward each other. An Isaac Newton watches an apple fall to the earth, and links the earth to a distant star. An Einstein takes the concept farther, deciding that matter itself creates a gravitational field by distorting the space around it, as a billiard ball resting on a rubber sheet

makes a depression in the sheet. A Madame Curie sifts
through a ton of pitchblende with her husband before
obtaining a few grains of a new element, radium,
marking a turning point in modern physics and leading
eventually to releasing the energy of the atom. A Ben
Franklin flies a kite and learns the power of electricity. A
George Washington Carver finds three hundred ways to
use a peanut! He discovers how to derive synthetic
marble out of wood shavings, and starch and gum from
cotton stalks. A modern-day hydrogeologist finds "waters"
stored deep in the desert since the Ice Age, and works to
free them so vegetables can be produced from the parched
sand. Endless resources, seemingly hidden by the Creator,
give to man the many rewards he can gain through
seeking and finding.

A third reason for Creation is *enjoyment.* God wants it to
be pleasurable for man and woman, who are His highest
order. There is to be beauty in the clouds, the rise and set
of the sun, the night sky; in the rain, the snow; in the
trees, the flowers, the grasses; in the streams and lakes,
oceans and islands. God intends for us to enjoy all these
through our visual sense and through every aspect of our
senses: through our ability to smell fragrant blossoms,
new-cut hay, ripe fruit, the sea breeze, food cooking;
through our ability to taste tangy grapefruit, crunchy
nuts, sweet sweet sugar cane, salt from the veins of the
earth itself; through our ability to experience the
sensation of touching skin, fur, bark, rock, mud, water,
grass, and the ultimate sensual delight that arises out of
human sexual desire. Through every human capacity we
are to *enjoy* Creation, in every way—with our intellects,
our spirits, our senses. Living is to be an enraptured
experience for us.

. . . charge them not to . . . set their hopes on uncertain riches but on God, who richly and ceaselessly provides us with everything for our enjoyment (1 Tim. 6:17, Amplified).

Yes, Creation in all its vast, extravagant array, is for us: that we may know God; that we may explore and master it; that we may find pleasure in it.

4. *He Needs Our Response*

Christ is the visible expression of the invisible God. He was born before creation began, for it was through him that everything was made.... In fact, all things were created through, and *for Him* (Col. 1:15, 16, Phillips).

Creation is for Christ: Is this a contradiction of our last chapter? How can this be?

Char and I were watching a sheer curtain of snow coming down, softening the harsh lines of stiff brown weeds and bare tree boughs. The next time we would talk, we knew that the Minnesota landscape would be greening with the life that insists on being displayed so jubilantly in spring. Those trees out there look dead now, yet we know that an invisible cycle of life continues: it comes and goes, comes and goes; seeds fall, sap rises, new life sprouts. Is it this mystery of life itself that is the evidence, or at least a part of the evidence, of "the power and divinity" so "plainly discernible, commonly seen," that Paul is moved by in his letter to the Romans? The continuing chain of life throughout history—is this the proof of divinity that can bring faith? The very life cycle that we count on to recur, year after year after year, turning with the seasons

throughout the days of our lives—is this clear enough to
bring faith?

It is certainly powerful. After the long dark and the deep
snows of winter, what does the warm kiss of the sun do to
me? The first robin? The early yellow defiance of the
dandelion? The gentle rain that forces green sprouts
even out of the asphalt or a rocky crevice? What do they
tell me?

"I've got spring fever today real bad!" we say.
One poet exclaims:

> Spring in the air.
> I am in love...
> My blood is
>   budding inside me!*
>
> *Nazim Hikmet*

Bursting from the very core of our own personal created
being surges the desire to love. Might this not be because
love is the essential quality of the Creator? And in our
crudest responses to the "power and divinity" that is
drawing us out of our wintry withdrawal, we extract
only a limited grasp of what's going on. We want to go
fishing, we say. We want to play baseball, tramp in the
woods, dig in the garden, make love, when what actually
is happening is way beyond any of those specific
pleasures. God Himself is calling us to a love experience
that is the jubilant and transforming fulfillment of our
meager lives.

---

*"A Spring Writing Left in the Middle," *Things I Didn't Know I Loved*
(New York: Persea Books, 1975), pp. 5-7. Copyright © 1975 by Randy
Blasing and Mutlu Konuk; used by permission of the publisher.

In the Trinity, out of love, God gifted His Son with a Kingdom. He gave Him all of Creation, including you and me. Creation is for Jesus Christ, yes; but then as part of that Creation, we are for Him as well. His need to love was there from the beginning, His need to reveal; but that loving also contained the desire that His creatures would be able to recognize the One who gave them life, and to respond to Him in love.

Love brought all things into being; and love it is that responds to the Being that brought it all into being. "Was it for Him, then, or for us?" We grappled with a flood of tumbling thoughts. Creation was for Christ, yes; but loving us, His ultimate Creation, He turns it all over to us—to satisfy our built-in hungers, for beauty, flavor, fragrance, spring, touch. He's fulfilling the yearnings of our seeking hearts by giving us things to enjoy. If there were nothing around us to reveal Him, if He were off somewhere in a void with no gifts to reveal His nature, how then could we love Him?

God has created man and woman with the capacity to respond to everything else He has created. We chuckled at the way this understanding was coming together for us: God creates all of this sweeping vastness: galaxies, oceans, deserts, mountains, grasslands, jungles. He appoints them with the stars, the moon, the cheery red cardinal, the delicate butterfly, the roaring beasts. Then He creates man.

Doesn't He have to be the One who put into man the capacity to appreciate, to enjoy, to desire, and to utilize all that He has already brought into existence? And at the same time He needs our response to it! We sat on the edge of our chairs shaking our heads. Wild, isn't it? We had come full circle.

5. In Outer Space

The sky was blue after the storm—polished blue. Its depth held me. I laid my book aside and stood up by the window. I was newly aware of what might be going on out there beyond the distance my eyes could see. *Until The Sun Dies,* a book by Robert Jastrow, a scientist and professor of both earth and space sciences, was expanding my world. I was muttering to myself about the galaxies moving at extraordinary speeds of 900 million miles an hour, when my wife, Ruth, walked by and asked, "Did you say something?"

Wearing my most obvious Mr. Tweedy smile, I turned around and stammered, "Those fellows out there on Palomar Mountain... do you realize... can you imagine... you know, the ones with that giant 200-inch telescope? Do you know what they're trying to do?"

Ruth looked puzzled, so I blurted, "They're actually trying to take a picture of the... beginning... of time!"

"What are you talking about?"

"Just that, honey. You know, the farther out in space we go, the farther back in time we go."

We both recalled the opening of the World's Fair in Chicago. It was common talk in 1933. A beam of light from one of the brightest stars in the Northern Hemisphere was captured to turn on the lights at the "Century of Progress." And it was a highly publicized fact that this star, Arcturus, was so far distant from the Earth that the beam of light had left that star thirty-three years earlier. Since then, we've been absorbed by science fiction stories about men who travel in space and come back years later, younger than they were when they were launched. And we've spent billions of dollars actually to place men on the moon and to rocket data-gathering equipment onto Mars.

When Ruth and I grew up, it was commonly taught that Creation took place in 4004 B.C. For years it was heresy even to open your mind to the possibility that God might be unfolding greater mysteries through the explorations of the scientists. Science, to the Christian, was a grim specter, threatening the very existence of God.

Yet as the years have passed, the explorations have continued. The earth and the universe appear to have aged incredibly since Usher set his date at 4004 B.C. And those of us who have made an effort to flex reasonably with new calculations find God getting larger and larger in our lives, not smaller and smaller, as we were told would happen.

My mind flashed on the description of "wisdom from above" as James defines it in his letter on practical religion in the New Testament: "Pure ... peaceable, gentle ..." he says it is. And then comes the shocker, *"open to reason ..."* (James 3:17, RSV).

James is suggesting that what man must do is keep an open mind, that there's no way to know all, to understand all. He infers that others are going to participate in the expansion of our concepts. He's suggesting, "Don't close yourself off. Don't close your system, your world. Keep it open for growth, for development, for participation, for further enlightenment."

Then James goes on to add, "full of mercy and good fruits, *without uncertainty*. . . ." The paradox of being "open to reason," and yet being "without uncertainty," has been a struggle for me. Now I've finally arrived at the place where I believe there is an area of certainty for all of us.

One of the reasons for the Incarnation—that tiny little bit of time that God spent on earth in the vast overall scope of history—was to give man enough certainty to go on. "God is still in control" is the message of the Incarnation; "He is with us." In the form of Jesus Christ He gives us a glimpse of certainty—enough to hang onto as we build our lives, but with the encouragement that there's more to be found.

I picked up Jastrow's book and started to read again:

> According to the latest measurements of the speeds and distances of the galaxies, the most probable value for the age of the Universe is nearly *twenty billion years.*

The biblical words echoed in my head: don't close your mind, just because you have some certainty; *live* in the area of certainty, but with an openness about all the rest that I want to pour into your life. I returned to Jastrow.

What is the meaning of twenty billion years? What is the meaning of one billion years? The mind cannot grasp the significance of such vast time spans. A million years seems like a very long time, but a billion is a thousand times a million. Nonetheless, nature requires this enormous number of years to create its great works. . . . The mind must stretch its concepts of time and space far beyond their normal limits to comprehend the sweep of the events that make up the history of our Universe.

Open to reason . . . open to reason . . . open to reason . . . open to reason . . .

Suppose we adopt a point of view so broad that the tremendous span of a galaxy seems a detail, and the passage of a billion years is like an hour. Imagine the face of a cosmic clock on which one twenty-four-hour day represents the life of the Universe. On this clock, one million years is a minute, and ten thousand years—the entire span of human civilization—is one-tenth of a second.

I was wide-eyed, almost breathless as his suggestions flooded over me.

Consider the great events in the history of life on the earth within the framework of that analogy. Let the creation of the Universe occur at midnight; then the galaxies, stars, and planets begin to form twenty minutes after midnight, and continue to begin to form throughout the night and day. At four p.m. on the following afternoon, the sun, the earth, and the moon appear. At 11:53 p.m., the fishes crawl out of the water; two minutes before midnight, the dinosaurs appear; sixty seconds later, they disappear; one second before midnight, modern man appears on the scene.*

---

*Robert Jastrow, *Until the Sun Dies* (New York: W. W. Norton, 1977), pp. 25, 26.

I closed my eyes and let out a low sigh. Without realizing it, I'd held my breath for the entire paragraph! In Jastrow's timetable man appears so insignificant. But wait! in the light of forever and ever and ever, don't we gain a tremendous amount of significance—appearing on His timetable just before the twenty-four hours are up? I'm feeling an overwhelming importance coming on the scene with the rest of humanity a second before midnight.

What does this mean in God's timetable? Has the stage just been completed so He can unfold *His* purposes? Was this entire display of the miracle of Creation a mere overture to the setting up of His eternal Kingdom? Is it reasonable? Does it make good sense that Creation is *for* Jesus Christ? That the Creator-Redeemer would create something for himself? With a beginning and an end? But that we are literally made for Him and will outlast this very Creation He took so long to produce? Oh, the majesty of the idea that we are worth all that time and trouble!

If the intricate process of creation required twenty billion years—or one billion (or even one million, as far as our ability to comprehend that kind of time span)—is that belittling God? Isn't it rather adding immensely to His magnitude? To consider that all this time and energy was focused on setting the stage for us who are made in His image, drew me to a surge of adoration I had never known. Only Handel's magnificent "Hallelujah Chorus" could match my sense of jubilation! I pawed through the records, and listened spellbound to the "forever and ever and ever and ever."

Once created in the image and likeness of God, man doesn't take long to run into difficulty. Almost immediately we're up to our ears in trouble, to the point where we need help from heaven. "Help! God, help!" Then in the midst of this tiny speck on the timeline, God arrives.

In that minuscule period, God comes to bail us out. He tries to rectify, to redirect, to get us back on track, to change our course to the correct one. He comes to provide another opportunity for us to use our free will to get back into the act in the way He wants us to be. Then, with the promise, "I'll be back so we can really enjoy it all together," He leaves . . . with the reminder that we need not worry!

The entire Incarnate rescue is only a little "beep" in all of time!

It was several days before I could verbalize any of the cometlike thoughts that streaked through my mind as I read that book. What was so phenomenal for me was to put into Jastrow's time frame the idea of the Incarnation. The perspective is enormous: that after billions of years of preparation, God himself appears, and in that tiny fraction of time, just prior to the clock running down, He redeems man. *He makes all the difference!*

I look for Him to come again, and when He does I expect that He will redeem the whole of creation—not just the human part, but everything that preceded us. The earth does groan. This planet, this little gemlike sphere of blue, with tints of green, russet, and gold, waits for that point in time when God will reenter. None of the other planets moving around our sun is so beautiful, says Jastrow.

But I don't ever want to forget this: Whatever happens in between His comings He has left to *us!* He trusts us with everything here. After His momentary intervention on earth He departed . . . *and we are in charge!* We are expected to participate in this flabbergasting program of making men and women whole.

I get the feeling of awe, yes, but it begins to expand for me the crucial nature of our human role. For the first time I get an inkling of the huge, very huge part God asks us to play. He brings us into His creation wanting to share it with us—the marvel, the beauty, the wonder of it all. He wants us to participate with Him in this grandest of all schemes. But more than that, He can't make it go without us! To make it go He *has* to have the men and women, boys and girls, who choose to share in His plan. He gets those into the act who are capable of enjoying the magnificence. We've got it in our hands!

If history is all pointing toward one point, it isn't midnight, Mr. Jastrow, it's the kingdom of God dawning. All of this 20-billion-year time span has been set up for the establishment of the Kingdom of God on earth. All of the passage of time that the human race embraces is a mere speck in the whole scenario. You'd miss it if you weren't looking. It would all be past, and you wouldn't have recognized the crucial point of all creation. Creation is the stage for His kingdom! And that kingdom will be forever.

Oh! The splendor of it! Here it took a man whose life is devoted to scientific discovery, not a theologian, to help me gain a perspective of the overall plan of the Omnipotent.

In the mind of the scientist, all of creation is winding down. But at the same time Jastrow is elated to suggest that the galaxies may keep regenerating. It's distasteful even to the astronomer's mind to consider that the universe has an end. He is on a continuing quest for eternity. What is all this for?

It's part of whatever is to be. With God, Creation is an ongoing, forever-and-ever work. If He cares to create another sun He will do it. If our sun dies, which science expects it will in another six billion years, what are our prospects? Maybe we'll move on to another world where climatic conditions are just right, to stay there till that sun dies. Then we will move on to the next one. I want to be part of that kind of space travel that will happen without rockets or satellites or compression chambers. For when we are caught up to meet Christ in the air, literally, who knows what suns will just be born, and what new worlds will start to spin?

I suspect that Jastrow may be right so far as the age of the earth is concerned. That seems to be fairly well documented now. The Christian can relax; I don't think we need to struggle any more. If that's the way God wanted to do it—terrific! It doesn't make any difference HOW God brought about Creation; He is its author, and that's what matters.

What *is* important is our response to Him. It's our
openness to Him that is important, our willingness to
trust Him, our readiness to be engaged in His operation
of the world here and now. He requires our involvement
with Him in every aspect of managing this fabulously
ancient and complex planet which He put together. You
and I are an essential part of it—a huge part.

It amazes me what Jastrow has pulled together. He's
exercising what I consider vision. He bases that vision on
certain particles of information and truth that have come
down to us. He puts it all together and gains a
perspective.

So little do we Christians do that! Our vision is so often
hindsight, with our heels dragging. Rarely are we out
front, wanting vision, wanting to be part of putting
people together so that great things can happen.
Enabling events to take place because we took some
initiative, saw some possibilities—for the future, for
mankind—some vision of what could happen if the
dynamics were right.

That's what Jastrow is talking about in the natural
scientific sense. And we who call ourselves by the name of
the Creator-Redeemer, what do we do? We have His gift
of the spiritual to expand us, to extend us beyond
ourselves; yet so often we are confined by it instead.
We're restricted to a small particle of truth—a speck of
certainty; and we're fearful of going beyond that speck
that we're sure about, to accept some other particle of
truth that is strange to us—found by someone else. "The

wisdom from above is first pure, peaceable,
gentle . . . open to reason."

It has always been a human tendency to snap shut
whenever we grab onto some bit of certainty. We leap to
protect it, enshrine it. It is the rare person who makes the
effort to *live* in the area of that certainty, who stretches to
its boundaries with an openness about all the rest of truth
that God wants to pour into us out of His limitless self.
The stage has been built. The drama can go on. You and
I are the players. Incarnate. Flesh-and-blood containers
for Almighty God!

6. *Limits*

The rim of mountains totally surrounds us in this familiar wooded village. Yet even in their enclosure, we comment on the spaciousness of the west country, as though the limitation of the rim itself makes the space more observable.

The rhythm of our days is alternating here; from the enormous display of natural wonder which always fills us in this place, we are caught up in a continuum of new and dire demands. From the shiny vastness out of doors we slip quietly into the smallness of a dim room. There we focus all our energies on the highly prized life so suddenly being crushed out of Dad's cancer-ridden body.

We have come home, all of us children, to be reunited with our parents, aware that Dad could be taken from us at any time. We are five grown men—brothers—and our one sister. Leaving the familiarity of our own individual families, we sense a goodness in coming together, once again into the old circle; yet it is strange. It is not normal. Not one of us can escape the grievous certainty that death has yanked us from our present roles; and with Dad's last rites completed, we will scatter over the country, back to the spouses, sons and daughters, and callings, that give us identity and meaning.

Outside the door we gasp the clean air, sing in the warm sun, absorb the liveness of giant pines, slender aspens, a chipmunk streaking under the steps, deer grazing across the road. At night, the intense darkness invites so many stars—and clusters of stars—to look down, that I am lifted into the magnitude of the universe.

Even with the love that drives us, it is still hard to leave the vast spaciousness and come back into the enclosure of the bedroom where life and death grapple in Dad's body. It seems a trap. Both he and I want to spring it—I know that—and get on with the business of living. We'd like to be done with this ebbing drain on our hours and days.

All of life seems focused onto this single point in time and space, using up all I can give. Far more consuming than any theatre stage is this frail human body where life exits. Dad is the star, and we the supporting cast. My arms become the strength that moves him; my eyes tell him what is going on in his reduced world; my hands on his back become his comfort; my presence his constant desire. My vitality is an extension of life for this dying man who once cradled me in his arms.

To be relieved by "Sis" at the bedside is my constant hope. Then I walk again under the wide sky and am pulled in all directions. The sun, the space, the dynamics of the early winter world refresh me. I draw in the fullness of God revealed to me everywhere.

The smallness I feel returning to the deathwatch is uncomfortable.

At some point in the extended quiet, however, it occurs to me how drastically the Creator had to "small down" every aspect of his being in order to be born in a manger. How else could he fit into the body of an infant, growing up on one limited segment of the beautiful but stubborn planet He designed, created, and dressed with people?

When I try to imagine the immeasurable transition He made, my own distress at leaving the mountain vastness for the confines of the bedroom seems petty. He was used to inhabiting all of infinity, yet His love for His creatures caused Him to telescope whatever divinity was needed into the limited frame of a human, an Earthian on his own Earth.

II. *God Reveals His Love in Jesus Christ*

7. Definitely Human

It was one-thirty as I roused from a sound sleep. At first I
didn't know where I was, or if I was dreaming. Or was
that faint sound someone calling for help?

As I reached for the light switch, I remembered I was on
the sixth floor of a big downtown hotel, where I had been
part of a Young Life Conference. It had been a
marvelous evening; the Spirit of God was very present.

"Help! Help! Help!" The sound returned much louder.
No, I was not dreaming. The voice was right outside my
door: "Somebody call the police."

I pulled on my trousers and stood there with my hand on
the chain lock. Should I, or shouldn't I?

"Help!" What is going on? I eased the door open and saw
two figures. It can't be. Yes, it is. A man is gathering a
sheet around himself with one hand; and a woman is
hanging onto him like an angry wildcat, trying to yank
some dollar bills out of his other hand.

I stood in the doorway with my mouth open—which wasn't very helpful; but before I could register what was happening she tripped him and he fell at my feet. In his effort to catch his balance he lost the sheet. And suddenly I was looking down on this weird scene—a fully clothed woman straddling a stark naked man who kept hollering, "Somebody help me! Help me! Help me!"

Meanwhile, up and down the corridor, doors opened, then closed. Across the way a woman stepped out, gasped; then her husband elbowed her back through the doorway. "Get back in the room, honey; get back in there."

All of us were watching, too incredulous to take any sensible action, when we saw the man flip his assailant over onto her back and pin her to the floor. Now he was astride her, and she was pouring out obscenities. The money lay scattered over the carpet.

"You cheated me out," she screamed. "I'm not gonna leave this place with a lousy three bucks!"

From the snatches of dialogue I pieced together a possible story. This evidently was her business. He apparently had signed her into the hotel, perhaps as his wife. Then when he had had enough and wanted to get some sleep, he tried to kick her out. She was outraged, and was going to at least put up a good fight for her full fee. All the while the man kept calling, "Help me."

The fellow in the next room stepped into the hall long enough to see what was going on. In a tone such as one might use to ask Room Service to send up a pot of tea, he offered to call the house detective. I stepped inside my room, closed the door, and leaned against it, shaking my head and muttering to myself, "How absurd!"

Lying in bed again, wide awake, the whole parade of impressions from the evening tramped across my mind. There was the great spiritual moment we had shared during the conference. That was real. And there was the wild, boobish scene in the sixth floor hallway. That was real. I started to laugh so hard I couldn't stop, it was so comical. Then I almost cried, it was so sad.

"But it's life," I insisted out loud. "It's the way life is!" Here is a woman, a unique person made in the image of God, selling herself to a stranger who is too drunk to appreciate her or care at all about her needs. Then he hands her three dollars and tries to send her on her way. "Holy smokes!" I sat right up in bed. A whole new insight opened in the darkness.

During the evening I had tried to share with the Young Life committee men and women, what it means to be "incarnational." I had spoken about the willingness of our Lord to reduce himself to being human—to strip himself of all divine privilege so he could enter our arena of living. That's what incarnation is: God becomes human.

Human? I saw clearly the image of the naked man losing his sheet. He was definitely human. I felt his need. I felt her need. I felt the drives the Creator had built into them in the first place. In disbelief I thought: in order for the Creator to become the Redeemer he had to take on all our weaknesses, our needs, our absurdities—as well as our strengths. The Creator stripped himself of all privileges and became a human creature such as we are. I stared at that image, still vivid on my brain—that defenseless man, totally stripped, stark raving nude. He had nothing to hide behind.

It boggled my mind. O, dear God. We hide behind anything we can latch onto: titles, clothes, programs, degrees, experience or lack of it, good works. And You gave up everything to become human.

Then that "everything" started gathering meaning. I realized I had no idea of what He gave up. I couldn't in my wildest imagination begin to grasp the feeblest inkling of what it was He left behind, of what the other side is like. I only saw what I hide behind to keep from being stripped, so I won't be empty, so I will look good.

The scene outside my door was a great skit I'd been shown. God has to have a beautiful sense of humor. The comedy of life was there right alongside the tragedy. "What a mix!" I exclaimed before I finally fell asleep. I know He sees it all: our beauty, our stupidity, our absurdity. He died for this. Funny thing, that He's willing to give Himself totally for this. . . .

I must not forget tonight. God is not only Spirit; God is *human* spirit. What is real? The moments we shared in the conference I knew were the real world; the real world is the world of the spirit. But powerfully superimposed on that peak spiritual experience are those writhing, hollering humans stripped of privilege. And I know this is real too! This is not unreal. This is the raw human stuff we have to deal with as we ask ourselves, "What does it mean to carry the life of God in us into today's world?"

8. In the Marketplace

While being human puts us in the highest order of
Creation, it is not always pretty. Sometimes we have to
confess to this very abruptly—and personally.

The marketplace in Baguio swarmed with Filipinos—solid
people curb to curb. I was entranced with the color: the
baskets, fruits, flowers, embroidery, tiny brooms, brass
work. Here, I was a foreigner, "Americano." Only just
that morning had we changed my dollars into pesos.

I hadn't even looked at them yet to figure out what was
what, when a very gentle touch on my arm swiveled my
head to the right. I was startled at the tiny brown woman
looking up at me. I smiled and turned back to my friends
who were bargaining for a beautiful rust-brown woven
bag.

Again there was a touch on my arm and again I looked.
No words passed between us. I was strangely nonplussed,
trying to comprehend my own ineptness. Obviously, I
had far more than she had, and my natural impulse was
to give something to her. The newly exchanged money in
my pocket felt like "Monopoly" cash. It had no value to
me; I didn't know one coin or one bill from another.

49

I turned back to my friends, but the repeated touch on my arm could not be ignored. Again I looked down at the tiny, little, shriveled, brown-faced, snaggle-toothed, quiet lady, marveling at her persistence. This time she motioned, with fingers clustered as though holding a piece of bread; she raised them to her mouth. She's hungry, I realized in embarrassment. Again, I smiled, stupidly, and turned away to follow my friends, who had completed their purchase and moved to the next stall. I dared not look back to see if she came with us.

For days that wrinkled old brown face flashed on the screen of my mind, that persistent person, asking, asking, asking—and not receiving.

In another marketplace, another era, another land someone asked and received, in quite a different fashion from the One who was human but also divine.

Man and woman, left alone with only the natural Creation around them, get into difficulty. They begin to destroy, to misuse, to abuse, to neglect or overlook, that which the Creator gives them to enjoy. With only the broad general sweep of Nature around them; without the understanding of the specific, the *Man* with a capital M, people are inept with each other. So the Creator comes into His own Creation to put it back together. The Creator becomes a creature in order to begin to rectify the wrongs, to reconcile His creatures back to Himself, to reconcile them to their environment, and to each other. He takes that which is highest in His created order, a human being created in His image, as His earthly form. He is born at a specific time in a specific place to show through this One human life how it is to live fully. He comes to His own created Earth to model human life, to put it into practice as He intends that life should be lived.

What this One human does is accomplished primarily by relating to the people around Him. The way He does this demonstrates something totally new to us—namely, what is good and what is bad. We, of course, have already made up our minds that we know this, but His definition is higher than ours; His thoughts, His ways, are startlingly different. Somehow, without Him around, we don't realize, or we forget, that the essence of life is found in the "other," that it is in living for the other and caring for the other that life comes alive.

He comes among us and cares for people: sick people, poor people, alone people, rejected people, oppressed people, misused people. Wrinkled, shriveled, snaggle-toothed, hungry, elbow-high people. All of these He relates to as vital, important individuals, significant not only to God but to each other.

These people, he indicates to us, are exactly what will *make* life for us; they will begin to correct the ineptness, the defects of life in us. We each have a part to play; in caring for "others" as significant creatures of Almighty God we begin to fill in the little gaps in each other.

That was the Creator-Redeemer's purpose in joining His creatures on Planet Earth, to reveal something by relating to us, right here in the marketplace.

"For God so loved the world that He gave His Son . . ." has been so often quoted that the love it expresses suffers from glibness. It was Love that motivated the entrance of Jesus Christ into our human sphere. It was Love that He came to show in specific ways with specific people. It was Love He demonstrated again and again in the midst of problems: in solving the stupid, thorny dilemmas of everyday people who stray from the norm of life; in breaking down walls so petulantly built between people. He sat with the woman who came to the well for water; He caught up with the woman taken in adultery, after the righteous churchmen had dropped their stones; He walked up to the blind man sitting by the roadside. In all these and many more specific situations, He was revealing in a very here-and-now manner the amazing changes that occur when we care about each other's lives.

One day, leaving Jericho, this God-man stops in front of a blind man and asks, "What would you like me to do for you?"

What a question! The *Creator* of the entire universe is standing in front of a beggar, asking him, "What is it you'd like, son? Let me know what I can do for you." That is overwhelming to me.

The blind man, who was calling out from the crowd, "Jesus, Son of David, have mercy on me!" is suddenly the sole object of attention of the One who put the worlds together!

The crowd had been trying to hold him back, "Knock it off. Keep quiet back there!"

But Jesus says, "No, bring him on in. C'm'on over here." And they told him, "It's O.K., Bartimaeus. Come on. He wants you."

The blind man threw off his coat, jumped to his feet, and came right up to Jesus. And just as if no one else was there, Jesus asked him, "What would you like me to do for you?"

Immediately Jesus focused on that one person, gave him His total and complete self. Nobody else that we know of was asked that question that day in that place. According to the record there was only one person in that crowd who was really crying out for His help. Bartimaeus had a need, and he sensed that his need could be met by this Person coming down the road, so he directed his request to him, "Jesus, have mercy on me." Jesus responded and made it just as personal, "What do you want me to do for you?" What a loving act that was!

The request of the man was direct, to the point, "I only want my sight, that's all. If I could just see like most people."

And Jesus, happy to do so, gave it to him.

Simply and basically the story illustrates *how to love.* A man in need asks, and because He asks of the One where love resides, he also receives. I had been gnawing on this for some time, that love is the pivot on which everything else turns. Love doesn't wait till Jesus enters the human scene. The fact that God *is* love pushes us way back to the beginning, and the revealing of God through Creation as an act of love. He's revealing Himself to us, because He's wanting to be loved back. So the whole idea of the highest order of Creation is to create someone who can share it all with Him. He makes us, male and female; He gives us everything to manage, to enjoy, to reveal His love; all the time wanting us to be led back into loving Him through all He has made.

Somehow we get off the track, so He sends a more explicit expression of His love. He puts His love in human form, so we can more closely scrutinize what love is, how love acts, what love does. He demonstrates in every instance that love is caring about another, love is reaching out of oneself to help another.

The leper looks at Jesus with piteous eyes, and out of his leprous condition, says, "If you want to, You can make me clean."

Jesus stretches out His hand and puts it on the leper and says, "Of course, I want to. Be clean."

Oh my! It just tears my guts out when I realize that the only Clean One in all of the world reaches out to identify with this unclean one (as He does also with the prostitute or any of the others) and *He touches that leper.* It's the clean one who takes the initiative. Goodness always reaches out. Love is always on the offensive. Love is never retiring, never backwards. It is love that extends itself; it is fear that holds back.

In all of His loving, His extending, His reaching out, He is appealing to us; and the natural human response is to love Him back. If we make this response, our priorities and values begin to line up in their proper order, and they fall into their proper perspective for us. Our loving back begins to make life function right, the way He means it to function, and in that proper functioning we begin to get personal health. We begin to like ourselves better; we begin to have enough strength to reach out and kind of fearfully try loving each other a little bit. And all the time we are adding additional health to the earth. We are correcting the ill of the sickness of the world, because we are getting the love back in!

When I think of this side of God—willing to reach out, to stretch out, to empty Himself so He can come and be filled with whatever is necessary so the world will know that He does indeed care—this it is that enables me so much better to understand the Cross, and why Christ was so totally rejected.

God is so extremely vulnerable to human error that He is even willing to be killed. But because He is love, He also knows that Love cannot be killed—instead it spurts out in another direction. It's like trying to stamp out the mercury on the floor when a thermometer breaks. It can't be stamped out; it just spurts out into more and more mercury beads that scatter across the floor in all directions. Every time we hit Love, it spurts out in some other form. To me, that makes the Cross take on an entirely new kind of sense, because it wasn't only God dying for our sins in the old doctrinal sense, but it was His chance to demonstrate the indestructability of Love!

There is no way to destroy God, because God is Love, and Love never ends; Love cannot be put to death. You may kill an expression of it, but it will come out another way. It will come out in resurrection. It will come out in a woman who can walk away from her accusers, holding her head high, a new person, with a new identity. It will come out in an outcast leper, who becomes pure and whole and returns to an acceptable place in society. It will come out in a blind man who regains his sight, who can leave his roadside seat as a beggar and become a respectable citizen. God cannot die, because He is *Love*, and Love never ends.

That is precisely what creates hope in life. That is what creates brightness. That is why it's even all right to reach out to love and have your love rejected. When you reach out in the name of Christ, in a loving way, to the stranger in your midst, to the visitor in your house, to the beggar on the street, to your own son or daughter, and you lovingly give, it does not truly matter if your love is misunderstood or cast aside. Even when you are rebuffed, love is not defeated; it cannot be killed. Because it is love, it will come out some other way. What we are asked to do is to love; we may not ever see the results of that love in another.

Even more fascinating is the fact that in our loving, in our reaching out, we ourselves experience more of God. Why? Because we begin to see, to understand that what is happening is way beyond what we are conscious of doing. Already He is out there. He is in that person to whom we extend ourselves. He is waiting—always to meet me in that "other"; waiting—for me to treat that one with kindness and love so that He can respond to me.

9. *Messing Around with Bad People*

The Bible is a book for troubled people. Jesus came to make the broken whole. There is a story in the Gospel record that starts out, "... a bad woman found out that Jesus was there ..." (Luke 7:37). It says so much about those who think they are qualified, and those who don't appear to be qualified at all. Here it is in the Phillips version:

> Then one of the Pharisees asked Jesus to a meal with him. When Jesus came into the house, He took his place at the table and a woman, known in the town as a bad woman, found out that Jesus was there and brought an alabaster flask of perfume and stood behind him crying, letting her tears fall on his feet and then drying them with her hair. Then she kissed them and anointed them with the perfume. When the Pharisee who had invited him saw this, he said to himself, "If this man were really a prophet, he would know who this woman is and what sort of a person is touching him. He would have realized that she is a bad woman."

Well, of course. He did! That's the point.

> Then Jesus spoke to him, "Simon, there is something I want to say to you."

"Very well, Master," he returned, "say it."

"Once upon a time, there were two men in debt to the same money-lender. One owed him fifty pounds and the other five. And since they were unable to pay, he generously cancelled both of their debts. Now, which one of them do you suppose will love him more?"

"Well," returned Simon, "I suppose it will be the one who has been more generously treated."

"Exactly," replied Jesus, and then turning to the woman, He said to Simon, "You can see this woman?"

Jesus is asking Simon a question, "Do you see this woman?" He is not making a statement. He knew Simon couldn't see the woman; he was not able to see the potential of a person in her. Simon saw a prostitute, a social problem; he was seeing an intrusion that was raising havoc with his luncheon, and with his system. All his life, he has been part of an ecclesiastical system that taught him, "Don't mess around with bad people." And here is Christ demonstrating that that is exactly what God came into human society to do—to mess around with bad people; and Simon begins to detect it was not to mess around with good people, which is going to break into pieces the very system he is trying to protect. This woman is a threat to his system. Her coming into his house is going to make a bad name for him, while Christ, living on the edge of risk, is willing to have a bad name, or anything else, to get the truth out.

What an amazing picture this is! Here is Jesus at a respectable meal, in a respectable home; and this woman comes off the street, right into the dining room of this home where she's not been invited! You don't do that in an Oriental home! You don't do it in America either. This woman has broken with every tradition imaginable.

She defies the religious leaders by coming to see this upstart preacher whom they probably want to question about his doctrine. (For some reason they wanted to talk with him; I can't believe it was for any wholesome reason. I think they probably had some rationalistic, intellectual idea in mind—like most of us who "sniff each other out" theologically to find out where we stand.) Then this woman comes in and blows the whole scene. And what Jesus does is a mind-boggler.

Typical of whatever He does in life, Jesus takes a bad scene and makes a good one out of it. He then compares the Pharisee with the prostitute, the religious person with the "bad" woman. And she looks good and he looks bad.

> "I came into your house but you provided no water to wash my feet. But she has washed my feet with her tears and dried them with her hair. There was no warmth in your greeting, but she, from the moment I came in, has not stopped covering my feet with kisses. You gave me no oil for my head, but she has put perfume on my feet. That is why I tell you, Simon, that her sins, many as they are, are forgiven; for she has shown me so much love. But the man who has little to be forgiven has only a little love to give."

She was emotionally involved, wasn't she? There are so many beautiful clues here. The woman probably doesn't really understand what she's doing. She is coming to someone whom she suspects can help her. She's drawn to Him to express what she needed to express. She doesn't know how to do it. She's clumsy, she's awkward; but she is obviously prepared. She has the perfume with her for some reason; I'm sure it wasn't just to dab behind her ears. I don't think she predicted she would mess it up by crying; but her tears fall onto his feet, and she is down on her hands and knees caressing them, and wiping them with her hair.

The religious host must have been horrified! He thought he was doing a nice thing, inviting Jesus to a meal in his home. I'm sure he thought he was extending himself. He had gone out of his way; but in the process he had overlooked a few niceties. One, there was no warmth in his greeting. Simon gave himself away by a simple lack in his greeting. Simon didn't act like he really wanted to see his guest, and Christ took that personally. Two, there was no water to wash His feet. Christ noticed that this culturally proper welcome had been by-passed. Three, there was no oil for His head. Another usual courtesy is neglected. All of this 'little stuff' that expresses love to a guest is missing. So Christ turns around and says, "Simon, you flunked. The woman passed."

The comparison between the Pharisee and the prostitute begins to show how our ways and our thoughts are not His. He destroys the "religious" life this man had built up as his approach to God. Then He looks at the woman with her simple acts of love and says, "Your faith has healed you!"

That simple expression—was *that* faith? If we were to see Him, would those actions comprise saving faith for us?

The woman was terribly in debt to this man who accepted her, so her sin was obvious to her. She demonstrated that she was, indeed, a sinner. Simon's sin was obscure because he didn't have much of a need; he didn't really think of himself as a sinner. So Jesus dealt with the one

who knows her need, "Your sins are forgiven; your faith
has saved you. Go in peace." He gave her new life, *real*
life, because He always deals with the real world. The
reality in her case was her deep need to express her love.
Her need was no worse than any other need.

One of the things that has smitten me over and over
again is the fact that many of us don't really believe we're
sinners! I'm convinced that at some point I have to come
face to face with *my* sin, my own personal sin; and that sin
becomes apparent to me through some failure or
weakness of mine. Maybe it's a socially unacceptable act
we're drawn into. Maybe it's a political or financial
cover-up. Maybe it's an inept withdrawal from what we
know is right. Some way, somewhere along the route,
God is going to help us find out that we're sinners. We
show weakness. We mess up. We demonstrate we don't
have it. However it happens, this is an essential step in
our development as believers. The next step, and the
next step, and the next step all have to be taken. See,
there are any number of points that are necessary along
the way of life; and one of them is to confront how needy
we are.

Christ touched the woman in Simon's house, but that is·
only part of the impact of this story. I guess I'm sensing
that beyond *this* particular woman, or even the bigger
issue of prostitution, Christ was touching someone who
hurt, someone who was not acceptable to society, or to a
religious system. The story starts with "a bad woman. . . ."

We are constantly producing "bad people" in our world,
one way or another—through ignoring or neglecting each

other, or through doing something deliberately hurtful. We turn people off; we drive each other to do something that is not healthy; we overlook someone, or turn our backs on an obvious need; and the outcome is a "bad" person, or a "bad" social condition. That's what God came to deal with when He came into the world. Jesus Christ came to meet our "badness" head-on. The "bad" he can influence and change. The "good" He has to leave as it is, because it is self-righteous, and therefore unchangeable.

10. *Appropriate*

My young son Richie went with me to the supermarket
one evening. We were talking with the man behind the
counter when Richie said, without a touch of hesitation,
"Dad, I think you pray too long in family devotions."
Richie was ten.

The busy store seemed an inappropriate place to talk
about our spiritual differences, but I tried to set aside my
embarrassment sufficiently to be receptive. I was startled
by my own response to Richie's clean conclusion
reverberating in my mind: You pray too long. You pray
too long. You pray too long. Somehow I'd seen myself as
more open, more flexible, more accepting than this
incident showed me to be.

Following my initial surprise, and my sensitivity to the
man behind the counter, my next thought was to excuse
Richie. After all, he was only a child and had little
understanding of what was appropriate and what was
not.

Since then I have decided that Richie was the one who
behaved in an appropriate fashion. He was dealing with a

matter of great importance to us both, at the time it came to his mind. I was the one who had gotten "layered" over with the superficial "rights" and "wrongs" of my culture to the point that I was going to keep my marketplace conversations separate from those dealing with our spiritual formation.

"Appropriateness," as we practice it, is not determined by truth, but by culture. When we talk about something being appropriate, we're talking about what we have concluded is acceptable to society, and that will vary from place to place. We build little boxes within a society—what we consider appropriate "on the town" Saturday night is not appropriate for Sunday morning in church. And what's appropriate in church is not appropriate in the office or the factory during the week. When we strip aside culture and start dealing with candor, as Richie did, we find it's the truth that is crucial, and the time and place doesn't matter.

Do you remember the record of Christ coming into the synagogue and healing a man's deformed hand? (Luke 6:6-11). It was against the law in the Jewish culture to do any kind of work on sabbath days, and so on another occasion (Luke 14:5) Jesus confronted the Pharisees, "If your cow fell into a ditch on the sabbath, would you leave her there, or pull her out?" The account of the healing of the man's hand tells us that his candor turned his enemies "wild with rage" (Luke 6:11). Jesus cut through the layers of Jewish culture and tradition to state very clearly that what is crucial is to do good, to save life rather than destroy it, to do kind deeds—even when the law makes it inappropriate.

I don't believe Jesus was condemning the religionists.
What deeply disturbed Him was their indifference to
human need. They were bogged down in their concern
over appropriateness, and needed to be redirected to the
very quality of compassion that this religious life was to be
about. That healing of the man's hand could have led the
Pharisees back to a deep personal worship of the
Creator—God, the One who had created all of their
potential for wholeness—if only they had been able to
recognize the real issue.

Today our cultural systems are thick and overgrown. It is
extremely difficult to break through them. What *seems*
appropriate actually *becomes* appropriate in our behavior,
simply because the complexities are so vast. Truth is very
difficult to get at unless there is an openness of mind—an
openness to the idea that there is something more
appropriate than what we have learned to accept as
appropriate.

> But the wisdom that comes from heaven is . . . pure and
> full of quiet gentleness . . . peace-loving and courteous. It
> allows discussion and is willing to yield to others; it is full
> of mercy and good deeds. It is wholehearted and
> straightforward and sincere (James 3:17, TLB).

When I was a boy at home, Mother always wanted her
children dressed in white shirts when they went to
church. From her perspective, this was appropriate.
Gradually we began to associate the experience of God
with a certain type of clothes. This kind of façade and
these layers of custom build up, sometimes for excellent
reasons. Yet gradually the layers can become so thick that
they hide the reality of the matter. Many people who are

brought to church in white shirts ultimately cannot find the heart of the Gospel because they are so caught up in how they look for the occasion.

We have made it almost impossible in our day to think through all the layers to find any real issue. But when we do get far enough down to see it, we're aghast at what we've been missing. Or, at what it will take to let that discovery change our behavior. One begins to wonder how much of life is really like that. . . .

I dare venture that a vast amount of our living is done on the surface of this multi-layered system of appropriateness. That's the hypocrisy kids hate so. They see us building defenses around ourselves—flimsy excuses, layers of tradition to bolster our own acceptance by other people.

But come back a moment to the supermarket. Who is the man behind the counter? Who are these other people we assume may feel our conversation is inappropriate? What are we denying them as we bolster our acceptance in their eyes? Why are we limiting the possibility of their finding a new quality of life?

What may seem on the surface to be most inappropriate, may be the very missing piece of truth they're seeking at this point in life.

Most remarkable to me, however, is that a little child still opens the door. A son exposes these camouflaged areas of life to his dad. The ramifications are endless, aren't they?

III. God Reveals His Love through Us

11. Truth on the Golf Course

Golf was fun yesterday. I enjoy it. Just getting out in the country has a great effect on my person. I love to wander outside in the green world.

On one shot my ball was deeply embedded in the tall grass. My partner was off in the other direction. Being alone, I mumbled to myself, "Shoot! If I could have landed on that nice low-cut grass on the fairway I could've gotten a decent swing at my ball instead of being buried over here." I was figuring how to loft it back onto the fairway, when I got to looking at the grass. Hm! They're both grass; one just happens to be cut a little different. There's no difference in the substance.

A bird caught my attention as it flew over. It lit in a tree, and click! A whole series of relationships came together for me. The bird sits in the tree; the tree comes out of the earth; the grass comes out of the earth; I'm walking on the earth. I kicked at the turf around my ball and said to myself, "I come from the same dirt that the grass and the tree come from. And someday I'll go back to it."

At one point in my life, I was willing to settle for the fact that God loved the world, but that the "world" He loved wasn't really the "earth." It was a kind of human system that included the people and the kinds of behavior they get into that determines the course of their lives and the wider course of history. That definition was never satisfactory to me. So when J. B. Phillips came out with his down-to-earth paraphrase of the New Testament—"The whole world is in travail, like an expectant woman, just waiting for the day in which the literal earth realizes salvation"—I said, "Aha!" Redemption was not only a "his-'n'-her" plan for the human residents of Planet Earth, but the earth itself is loved by God. It will experience salvation too. When the trees, dirt, rocks, oil, water begin to realize their day has dawned, redemption will be complete.

God placed us in his intricately created earth to manage it. He gave us minds to discover, to invent, to devise with ingenuity. Everything is here for us—the sun, wind, rain, oil, minerals, water, soil, seed. We discover we can open up the surface of the earth and get coal out. We start to deplete the supply, so we go deeper and find oil. From oil we learn we can get gas, and we devise endless ways to consume that. Now we are frantic about these resources running out, and are searching for others. We talk about His Creation, and we boast about being on His team, yet for the most part we nonchalantly identify with the very system that is a mindless expression of greed, mismanagement, and plunder.

There is a balance in Nature, we know that. Mountains are related to clouds, clouds are related to deserts, deserts are related to animals. We see balance in plant life, in rivers and beavers, birds and mosquitoes. Remember when old Bing Crosby used to get on the media and talk about how much we need to preserve the "wetlands," so they can perpetuate the balance of Nature?

"Today most of the wetlands are gone," the Chicago *Tribune* reported, (December 11, 1979) in an article by John Husar, "Vanishing Wetlands Vital to Man." Much of the remaining prairie and wetlands is being hurried into development because of population demands. Scientists fear a profound effect on man if the wetlands go. They are convinced that marshes, swamps, bogs, and wet meadows perform critical tasks for the environment. They aid in keeping flood crests lower by storing excess water and releasing it slowly after the crests have passed. They help to recharge aquifers, keeping water tables higher. They serve as filters to clean silt from waters flowing into them. They help remove toxic metals, phosphates, and sulphates from water, and they improve the air we breathe by growing plants that release oxygen.

Some environmentalists estimate that a community would have to pay $50,000 an acre to replace the services that the wetlands perform.

"A study of Georgia's Alcovy River system showed water that was heavily polluted with human sewage and chicken offal could be designated clean after it has passed through 2.75 miles of swamp forest. . . . Water quality benefits there reach $1 million a year. A Florida study reported that a 1,500-acre marsh can use all the nitrogen and one-fourth the phosphorus produced by the sewage plant of a city of 62,000. Yet society still looks at quiet bottomland waters and sees 'just a swamp,' a cheap, $400-an-acre wasteland standing in the way of progress.

"Owners of flooded homes attest to the numerous housing developments placed on wetlands. 'Man, with his infinite wisdom,' said Illinois' DOC Director, 'acts as though he firmly believes that, regardless of how unique, fragile, or beautiful a natural feature might be, he can improve it.'"

Nature, now and then, does get revenge.

12. A Part of the Whole

Most people recognize the interdependency in Nature, of course, especially those whose flooded basements make them well aware of where their homes were built. Even though we violate the natural balance we accept the fact of it. A recent inventory shows a surprising interest among private landowners in protecting many of America's natural areas. It seems that many of them didn't know what they had. When informed, at least ten per cent expressed an interest in cooperating by donating or dedicating the natural areas on their property for preservation.*

But when we get to the human race part of creation what do we do?

So often we resort to an independent "guts-it-out," everybody-on-his-own kind of dictum. Push yourself. Misuse your body. Abuse your strength. Then, when the body doesn't perform as well as it used to, we look for some unnatural stimulus to keep going, and some other

_____

*Chicago *Tribune*, December 11, 1979, sec. 1, p. 8.

unnatural substance to shut us down. We push ourselves,
and others, to the limits. "Have a cup of coffee." "Can I
fix you a drink?" "Do you have an Aspirin?" Then in
comes Christ to look over the scene. He reminds us, "You
are not to be independent creatures. The old tough
American view of individualism, 'make-it-on-your-own'
and quit banking on each other, is just another unnatural
substitute for the interdependency, the inter-relatedness
I've built into your very core."

In the history of Young Life there's been a drive to go
out by yourself as "The Lone Ranger" to lick the world.
We go out to find these high school boys and girls, to love
them, and if possible to introduce them to Christ. We are
the strong individuals who go out into a community alone
to do the job. For Christ's sake, of course. People marvel
at this great committed youth leader who can do this. But
deep inside the question keeps nagging us, "How much
can I do on my own? Isn't there somebody else who will
share the load with me?"

The realization that you need somebody grows out of
your own experience of weakness, your own
inadequacies, and this leads to becoming very certain that
being made for each other is for real. I've learned that I
was not meant to be alone, and I've been lonely out there
bashing away.

When I resigned the presidency of Young Life after
thirteen years in a totally absorbing assignment, my mind,
my body, my system began to have a chance to work on
itself. I can feel, literally *feel*, a chemical process going on
inside me. I would never have believed it if someone had

told me I would be able to *feel* a difference, but I can *feel* changes taking place.

Eating food is different: suddenly I'm tasting. I have taste buds I didn't realize were there. I'm rediscovering little things that are supposed to be a natural part of life. Last night I was tasting a potato. I love baked potato, particularly the skin. Oh! I remember that flavor! And last night it was the same flavor I loved when I was a kid. I hadn't even realized I was missing it. I just thought my taste buds had changed as I got older, but that isn't true. And suddenly the ability to taste is back!

Sleeping is different: to fall off to sleep naturally is overwhelming, to be able to put my head down on a pillow, just to lie there and suddenly be gone! I usually pray a little as I lie there because it's an old habit, and I enjoy it. But for years I had sleepless nights. A lot of times it wouldn't matter; I could lie down and pray and think out eight hours of what I wanted to do the next day. I'd be ready to go, and excited—stimulated by plans, activities, people. But I'd have to be "pilled" up in order to carry it out. I didn't have any idea what that medication was doing to me; all of life was constricted. Suddenly everything is loosening up; the biological process is freed up.

My mind goes deeper; there is a more thoughtful process going on. I sense there's more control. Spiritually I can see. My whole outlook is changing. It's subtle. It's quiet. I feel I am coming out into a new place. It may not be observable to anyone else, but it is such fun for me to rediscover the little things that are in life.

It makes me think of Nicodemus and the struggle he had trying to grasp what Christ meant when He told him that "... a man cannot even see the kingdom of God without being born again" (John 3:1–7).

For me to have things slowly awakened, enlivened, literally feels like being reborn. I can see so much more of what Christ was trying to say to Nicodemus because it makes sense to me now. It goes way beyond what we think of as the "spiritual" level of life. It has to do with *every* level. The touch of God in one's life wakes a person up to everything in a fresh new way. There is an enlivening of the body, the mind, the emotions that have been deadened. They're being brought back to life. They're being born all over again.

I had no idea how bone-tired weary I was till my system had a chance to work on itself again. That dawned on me after one of our staff couples said to me, "You've got to come talk to our support committee about how *they* are Young Life!" At first I thought they were overplaying it. Then I surmised that what they might be missing was that same interdependence and interrelatedness I needed. So with their support group I talked about the many different gifts, talents, qualities needed to pull off our ministry with high school kids.

Together we looked back at Paul's discussion with the Roman Christians centuries ago: "For as in one physical body we have many parts ... and all of these parts do not have the same function or use, so we, numerous as we are, are one body in Christ ... and individually we are parts one of another—*mutually dependent* on one another.

Having gifts that differ . . . let us use them . . ." (Rom. 12:4-6a).

What a profound design for human need is the Body of Christ! That very inner cry of our hearts needing one another is what our Lord demonstrated here on earth—that we as people desperately need each other. We think we can get by, on our own, but we can't.

Toward the end of His time here our Savior was talking to Peter in the sense of, "I *need* you, Peter. I'll forgive you when you fail, but I need you. I need you while I'm here, and I'll need you after I'm gone. But I *need* you. I expect you to be a part of all that I'm doing. I'm willing to take time for you to understand how much you need me, and how we're related together; but you'll find out too that I really need you, and I want you."

From our perspective many years later, we can look back and see that Peter became the disciple through whom 3,000 men and women responded to the invitation to receive the Holy Spirit of God and the church took a leap forward; but Peter became that disciple out of his willingness to see that the Savior needed him.

One of the purposes of God coming into our earth in the flesh and blood of Christ is to reveal that as the Creator, God is tying everything back together again. We're all related because of our common origin. There is a chain of life. Animals need other animals. We need the animals, the plants. Frogs need insects. Birds need worms. We need each other. We need God. God needs us.

This process is meant to go on in that very fashion. By persisting in a proper interrelatedness, the creation process can continue. Through lack of proper relatedness hurt and deterioration occur. We drink too much and we suffer. We stub a toe and we hurt; our whole body is hurt. The rape of the land goes on and the whole international body is affected. We have a polluted lake, and that pollution affects us, just like overindulgence or a stubbed toe affects us. By hurting we know that something is wrong. If we don't hurt because we're unrelated or disconnected, then we pay no attention to the wrong and will take no steps to remedy it. Maybe a neighbor, or some person who works next to us is hurting. We may not know what's wrong, because we're disconnected or unrelated, but when we're around that person we, too, may experience a vague sense of discomfort.

The Creator-God intended for us to be connected to each other. On the stone tablets that Moses brought down from the mountain to Israel, He set down some basic rules. These were to help people care about one another as they tried to live by them. They were to give light and to make life work. He gave further instructions throughout the Old Testament that would help keep things in balance.

The Sabbatical Year was established so that every seven years there could be a redistribution of wealth and power among the people of Israel (see Lev. 25). In that way life need never become overwhelming for anyone. The Sabbatical Year was not only designed to help the poor, the slave, the debtor; it also was to help the rich, the

landowner, the merchant. The successful one didn't have
to worry about his possessions, because every seven years
he knew his accumulation of goods or authority could be
divided up and shared with those who had little or
nothing. Every one could start at Ground Zero again.
Debtors were to be freed from debt during the Sabbatical
Year; slaves were set free and were given a piece of
property of their own so they could have a fresh chance
at life. A redistribution of ownership was to be brought
into play. Whether a person had done poorly or well, at
the end of the seven-year period he could wipe the slate
clean and start over. Quite a game! Dump the board and
everyone goes back to Space One.

Is that a possibility for our system? How in the world
could we express that idea in our modern society? It is so
much easier to fall in with our present system of the "rich
get richer and the poor get poorer"; but in the process we
increasingly sense that both are edgy with an inner
reservoir of apprehension, and crime increases. In a
world of hunger and poverty in one hemisphere, and
inflation and greed in the other, we are stymied in our
need to express our interrelatedness, and we forget that
we have a common Father.

God set this pattern as far back as Creation, with the
participation of Adam and Eve in the ongoing process.

"Let us make a man—someone like ourselves, to be the
master of all life upon the earth and in the skies and in
the seas. . . . And God blessed them and told them,
'. . . Look! I have given you the seed-bearing
plants . . . and all the fruit trees for your food. And I've

given all the grass and plants to the animals and birds for
their food'" (Gen. 1:26-30, TLB).

When Christ came, God himself, making a further effort
to be known to His creatures, demonstrated the
interconnectedness of all creation in everything He does.

He demonstrated it when He walked on water. I don't
think He was just dazzling us with a miracle; He was
demonstrating something more. He was taking the
elements and talking about control. He was defying
Boyle's Law of Buoyancy. It was not a matter of his feet
displacing the water. He literally went beyond the
physical law to show us that there is an interrelatedness
between creation and the Creator. Somehow the
Creator-Redeemer understands more, that we have yet to
learn.

He did it again with life and death, through Lazarus, in a
remarkable way. I don't think He was merely performing
another miracle by bringing Lazarus back to life after he
had been dead four days. I believe He was showing us
that dust and people are related. We came from dust, and
to dust we go back. Christ was able to reverse that process
because He understood a higher law. All is related. It isn't
that the body and the soul are so very different. In death
people take on another form. They are part of the same
parcel. They are not disconnected.

He did it again when He took a little boy's lunch and fed
5,000 men and women, plus children. He was taking the
grain that grew out of the soil, that was worked into flour
and made into bread, and was feeding it to hungry

people. We take things out of the ground; we eat them
and they become part of us. They are not human, in
the sense that we understand humanity; but in becoming
part of our bloodstream, they demonstrate the
interdependency of that which is grown with that which is
human. A nonhuman entity enters into our humanness,
and becomes part of the human. Even that which is
animal, which we feel we must kill in order to partake of
it, is eaten as meat in its dead state, and becomes part of
life again in our humanity. This interdependency goes on
constantly back and forth.

Unless we block it.

Jesus came on the scene through the Incarnation to give
us a fuller view of God. It's got to be fuzzy seeing
everything only through Creation, even though Paul
holds us accountable to do so (Rom. 1:19). God gave us
an added view through Jesus Christ. The closer we get to
Jesus, the clearer the view becomes of the Father.

Another principle of the Sabbatical Year was that the
land was to lie at rest for one year out of every seven. It
was allowed to replenish itself. The need to replenish is
just as great as the need to produce. Are we humans that
different? My abuse of my body, draining off my
resources, and doing little to replenish them—what about
that? Unless we take cognizance of the "little red light"
flashing inside us and stay in the sack, get out in the sun,
rest one day in seven, spend three months on the beach,
take off some weight—we'll do the same thing to our
bodies as we do to the land. When we draw off resources,
without replenishing, not only do *we* hurt, but we affect

the rest of creation! We are a deterrent to the process of producing life, growth, happiness, health because we have damaged our own lives, and we are part of the whole. We have damaged not only our immediate loved ones—spouse and children—but the whole business.

As I allow myself to be replenished, I am feeling a renewal of life. I am a part of the whole scheme of creation. Suddenly now I don't care to push, where before, pushing was the normal way for me to live. It used to be normal to get up and do my push-ups and not even consider what I felt like. Now I've got time to think about how I feel.

I've known something was wrong. I'm sure everybody knows, really. I've despised taking pills. (You don't like yourself for that, for the fact that you think you need something.) I also knew things were going by so fast I couldn't remember who was at an event, or where things took place. For the most part, everything went by in a big blur. When I *could* remember, I never took the time to sit back and recall the memories—to dream about what occurred, to take things apart and evaluate them. Life should not be that way. We should not have that kind of jam-up occurring. When there is so much crowded together, it seems the overload triggers a runoff valve and we lose its value.

This jam-up is not uncommon with people who insist on staying busy all the time. A woman shared with me an experience of being invited to speak at a conference. The letter of invitation was a personal one, reminding her, "We worked together several years ago. . . . I stayed in your home. . . ." But she was not able to bring back one iota of recollection. She could not remember the man who wrote the letter—at *all*.

How much we must miss in the busy-ness of carrying out our jobs! Like the Roman governor, Pilate, who missed the whole essence of who Jesus was in the process of doing his job. His ability to perceive was blocked off by his habitual need to perform properly as governor. He missed the whole drama occurring in front of him. There was a real live scenario going on right there in his palace—about life, about *his* life—and he stood there and asked an academic question, "What is truth?"

Jesus stood beside him and said, "I was born . . . to bring truth to the world. All who love the truth are my followers" (John 18:37). Pilate could have reached out and touched the Creator! He could have touched the very origin of life! The governor sensed something, but custom took precedence over discovery. He disconnected himself with what was really going on. He went out to the people to discuss with them the traditional release of a prisoner at Passover. He refused to be involved with the essence of what Jesus was saying. He preferred to play a head-game and ask, "What is truth." He decided to play it like a Roman in a foreign province, who didn't belong there, when he could have reached out in a simple human act, and laid hold of Truth itself.

Being willing to struggle with his personal conviction that Jesus was "not guilty," that he was a "good man," could have led Pilate to some further investigation. He could have said, "I feel you are here because of some jealous attack, Jesus, and I don't agree with these people, but I can sense I'm a part of what's going on. Caesar sent me. God sent me? I haven't liked it, but I do want to know what you're talking about." Performance of his role as governor, however, left Pilate little room to consider any personal curiosity or exploration. He had no concept of his own relatedness to any of it.

We talk about truth as an abstract. Truth is not abstract. It was personalized in Jesus Christ to demonstrate that there are absolutes. We can see them, follow them, understand them, grasp them physically as well as mentally. They are to be lived. That's why God made his second effort to reveal Himself—incarnate in human form. If He had not come here to live truth, how could we ever grasp it? We are not simply the Body of Christ, we are the embodiment of Truth in this world!

Yeah, I can identify with Pilate—busy carrying out his job, and disconnected from the truth in front of him waiting to be dealt with. . . .

13. *The Choosing Process*

"No man is an island," John Donne wrote two hundred years ago. Much longer ago than that God saw that it was not good for man to be alone, so he made Eve for him. The totality of Scripture from then on is the story of human beings and their dealings with each other and with their God. Your life and my life, and the way we feel about it, is still pretty much the result of the sum total of our relationships. The people whose lives are interwoven with ours can lift us to the heights of confidence and accomplishment, or plunge us to the depths of despair.

An intricate, invisible device at the heart of each human being nudges us in one direction, then another, in a never-ceasing effort to make personal contact. Watch a toddler in a waiting room find another child; he has no idea why he has to go "see the baby." Do you know why you have to call someone up to have lunch, go golfing, come for the weekend—or just talk? It's a tough thing to try to think about. Sure, you call a friend; that's what you do with a friend. But why do I *need* a friend? What makes me *need* to reach out of myself to relate to someone else? Why can't I just be by myself tomorrow and tomorrow and tomorrow?

One contemporary author says,

> We need other people, not in order to stay alive, but to be
> fully human: to be affectionate, funny, playful, to be
> generous. . . . Unless there is someone to whom I can give
> my gifts, in whose hands I can entrust my dreams, who will
> forgive me my deformities, my aberrations, to whom I can
> speak the unspeakable, then I am not human. . . .*

From our earliest efforts to find those who are the right
people for us, we enter into a process of choosing one
person, and leaving another out.

A small girl talked quietly in the bedtime dark with her
mother, "Let's invite Peter and Meggan and Donnie and
Holly to my birthday party."

"What about Kim?"

"No, not Kim." That was it. The matter was closed. She
had made her choices.

As children grow up they are learning there are "some
kids I get along with, some I don't." It doesn't mean the
ones we don't get along with are unattractive to other
people; there's just some reason that they don't click with
us. "She loves me, she loves me not . . ." and the search
goes on. Are we adults any different? In his quaint,
nineteenth-century way, Ralph Waldo Emerson
attempted an explanation: "Persons are love's world. . . .
Love is our highest word, and the synonym of God . . . a

---

*Hugh Prather, *Notes on Love and Courage* (New York: Doubleday,
1977), p. 2.

private and tender relation of one to one, which is the enchantment of the human life."* We'll do almost anything to gain love in some form, to draw someone else's attention to ourselves, and their approval.

Life is a network of personal relationships, interaction, interdependency, efforts at communication and understanding. All of life is a choosing process. The addition of people into our personal sphere *is* the human experience, whether those we choose have a positive or a negative effect. The negative effect, we know from experience, may add as much learning as the positive. When "Kim" doesn't get invited to the party, that's the lifelong selection process at work. When "Peter and Meggan and Donnie and Holly" *do* get invited they are *chosen,* and there is a tiny beginning experience of loving that starts functioning for them. Loving begins in making friendships at the simplest level.

Friendship is a form of love, a degree of love. On the ladder of life friendship is one of the rungs we begin on. We learn this *philos* love early. One child is attracted to another because they both play ball, or soccer, or clarinet; or perhaps they both take ballet, or go to the library, or are in the same Sunday School class. They like each other, but part of that liking is simply that they like to do the same things. They're thrown into the same situation; they exist side by side, day after day, in the band, the team, the class, and this forms the basis of interest to start something more going.

---

*Essays (New York: Clark, Given, and Hooper, n.d.), University edition, pp. 105, 106.

In *The Four Loves*, C. S. Lewis observes, "We picture lovers face to face but friends side by side." It happens all the time: the neighborhood, the school, the church, a circle of friends, the club form the matrix for the selection process to take place. Out of that side-by-side "situation" or common "interest" children are already taking some people in, and excluding others. In that way they are building their lives.

Later on there arises an invisible but compelling attraction—some people call it "chemistry"—between certain individuals. Who has ever been able to define this mysterious element adequately? Better writers than we have taken a stab at various aspects of it, or omitted it entirely. Years ago Emerson made this effort:

> The rude village boy teases the girls around the school-house door; but today he comes running into the entry, and meets one fair child arranging her satchel: he holds her books to help her, and instantly it seems to him

as if she . . . was a sacred precinct . . . and these two little
neighbors that were so close just now have learned to
respect each other's personality.*

During adolescence we see this so-called "chemistry"
erupting in a flood of new feelings and emotions, which
necessitate a more careful choosing. Suddenly, what has
always been simple attractiveness now leads to sexualness.
What I often see around the country is that some
teenagers at this point are so incapable of being satisfied
by the elementary aspects of becoming sexual that they
must devour each other. Wisdom flounders in the
biological urge. There is no sense of patience, of
deferring the complete sexual fusion to a more mature
time. They want everything *now*. Part of that is
characteristic of adolescence, and part of that is caused by
the time in which we live. From the day they are born
they breathe the idea of instant gratification. They are
immersed in a sea of production that promises
satisfaction. "Attract him with your perfume, your
lipstick, your shampoo, your toothpaste, your deodorant,
and you'll get him!" If you're taught that's what life is all
about, then when you smell sweet and look beautiful, and
some "he" finds you attractive, BAM! You've done it. It
worked. Why not merge? What else is there?

The other evening after we had finished dinner in a
restaurant, the young waiter came back to the table and
asked, "Would you like anything else?" One of the
women asked, in her natural warm, smiling way, "What
do you have?" And he answered with only an instant's
hesitation, "We have coffee and dessert . . . and my body."

Essays, p. 107.

That is so much a part of the culture today; I can offer
my body casually to anyone. The price is almost the same:
coffee, dessert or my body. The response is so natural,
right beneath the surface. All we have to do is trigger it.
When I talk with the girls at the Young Life camps on the
Christian view of sex and marriage, they want to know,
"How far can we go? To be popular you've gotta go to
bed with a guy."

"Who wants to be popular?" I ask. "Is that what you want
out of life—to be popular? Or do you want the *best* out of
life? What are you looking for? If that's what it takes to be
popular, and you want that kind of popularity, then go
after it. But I can tell you what you're going to do to your
life, in all likelihood." One girl came to me afterwards
and said, "I was so grateful you said that God forgives
us—that He can forgive and forget. Perhaps *we* will
always remember, but we *are* forgiven . . . and we can
start over. I want you to know that you gave me new
hope." And she walked off.

The potential for burnout is so real in those early days
when the sexual drive starts to make its demands. Before
young people are mature enough to get the fulfillment of
the experience, they are apt to burn out all the goodness,
the brightness, the aliveness, the hope and the
expectation. Instead of being the crowning act that brings
new life into the entire relationship it becomes a dead
thing—sickening, repulsive, boring. A bright young man
in New York told about a creative writing class in his high
school in which the members of the class began to share
their feelings through poetry. This led to intensely
intimate expression, which led further to sharing
sexually.

"Eventually nothing was too bizarre for us to try," he said. "I got to the place where I was so sick of sex, I never wanted to hear about it again. I was burned out before I left high school."

In this case the young man decided deliberately to close the door on the sexual because he wanted to make room for experiences in other areas of life. He chose to become chaste, at least for the time.

There is no value in chastity, however, when it develops out of a selfish or fearful choice to escape intimacy or human interdependency. A turning away from sex must be more than a refusal or denial. It should not create a void. Rather than only turning away from the sexual, chastity is meant to enable a turning *toward* something more appropriate, something more desired. It's a setting aside of one thing so there is room for something else to occur—whether it's in the context of marriage or singleness. What you do is consciously close one door so you can open another, one that is more appropriate. This choice can be made for life (as in the case of a religious celibate), or it may be made only for a period of time (as in the case of the young New Yorker, or as in marriage, with mutual consent, e.g., after childbirth, surgery; or it might be so that both partners can give themselves "more completely to prayer," as in 1 Cor. 7:5).

This sexual appeal that calls two people together is a significant power. It rises on cue during puberty, along with other changes, so that a boy and a girl can be interested in each other, so they can practice "loving" (not having intercourse, but being concerned with, caring about someone other than themselves). Adolescence is a prime time to be around enough boys and enough girls, on unpressured terms, to become comfortable with them as people. It's a time to begin to see that some things please them that don't please you, and vice versa. Some things you enjoy immensely may scare them half to death, or bore them terribly.

There is a force far deeper than sex at work in us, demanding attention, but so often people don't even know that! And they forfeit a mature love for the wild horses of the sexual drive that drag them off unprepared. In the instant gratification of the sexual clamor, so much of the loving process is lost. The learning to care about another person's *life* is blotted out in a few clumsy moments.

I'll never forget the day I handed a very close friend of mine an article on sex. I thought it was quite good. She started reading it and burst into angry tears: "Why doen't anyone ever tell us how to have *good* sex, instead of always telling us *not* to have sex." It must indeed be a cruel cut to many young people who are drowning in this societal sea, heaving with sexual overtones, to be told, "Cool it! Wait! Don't get involved sexually!" It's almost like telling a fish not to drink the water he lives in.

God made us to be sexual beings; and He designed our sexual sharing to be an ecstatic awakening, enlivening, renewing, and nurturing experience. It is meant to help us cross over the boundaries of our own selves and merge with another "self" in a miraculous time of mutual yieldedness and expansion. But for the sexual to be all of *that* it needs to be played out in the context of a mutual struggle toward growth and maturity—and all the rest of life. Part of the beauty of the *eros* kind of love lies in the way it can enlarge our capacity to be sensitized to another—*if* we're willing to work at it. To learn what it means to give to someone else, to learn how to yield our will to the will of another, really does take working.

The sexual is given to us to help us demonstrate what already exists in a relationship between a man and a woman. When very little exists, then only a very elementary sexual expression is fitting. It takes a lot of time to learn to care; it even takes a lot of time to find out what another person needs to have cared about! That's why marriage is the God-ordained framework for the sexual process, because it is a total commitment to care.

Years ago when I was studying, trying to get a handle on these matters for myself, I settled on some guidelines for behavior. As far as the faith is concerned it appears we "can do anything" (1 Cor. 6:12, Phillips); but there are three guidelines which the Apostle Paul gives regarding our general behavior and its effect on (1) ourselves, (2) the "others" in our lives, and (3) on God. I have used these often since then talking with both kids and adults.

To illustrate the first guideline I usually take a hypothetical situation: Suppose you're on an island by yourself. There is no other man, no other woman anywhere; you are alone, completely. What can you do? In 1 Corinthians 6:12 Paul shares two things regarding the effect of our behavior on ourselves: (1) "I can do anything I want to if Christ has not said no, but some of these things are not good for me"; and (2) "Even if I'm allowed to do them I'll refuse to if I think they might get such a grip on me that I can't easily stop when I want to" (TLB).

The first thing then is: *consider your own good.* Don't choose to do anything that isn't beneficial for your own self. This means you have to exercise your own mind and your own will. You are the one who has to take an active part in this choosing process; you can't simply stand by and watch God make all your choices for you. You are the active initiator of a plan to stop what's not good for you, whether it's eating chocolate brownies every day or masturbating every night, and to begin to do what will keep the Creation process flowing within your own supremely valuable self.

The second thing is: *consider what will enslave you.* Don't let yourself become locked into anything. Clothes. Cars. Girls. Boys. Athletics. Grades. Success. Cigarettes. Drugs. Beer. Television. Bridge. House and garden. You name it! Any enslavement is detrimental because it undermines your higher good. If we are to be enslaved at all it is to be to our God, because He is our highest good. He calls us to our best, and anything that robs us of that best must really trouble Him. So much for the effect on self.

The second guideline is becoming aware that *we live in community.* Once we can grasp the supreme value of our own selves, we can get off that hypothetical island and recognize that in real life we are never truly alone. Paul says: "Don't think only of yourself. Try to think of the other fellow, too, and what is best for him" (1 Cor. 10:24, TLB). There's no way out of it. We are not in isolation. We

are with other people and whatever we choose to do
ripples out to affect them. If I really want to follow Christ
in obedience, then no matter where I am I will begin to
choose to take consideration of my "neighbor," that
immortal "other" close to me.

Leading into the number three guideline, Paul
second-guesses our natural response to number two (1
Cor. 10:29–33), TLB, emphasis mine): "But why, you may
ask, must I be guided and limited by what someone else
thinks? If I can thank God . . . and enjoy it, why let
someone else spoil everything just because he thinks I am
wrong? Well, I'll tell you why. It is because you must *do
everything for the glory of God,* even your eating and
drinking. So don't be a stumbling block to anyone. . . .
That is the plan I follow too. I try to please everyone in
everything I do, not doing what I like, but what is best for
them, so that they may be saved." (In other words, so that
they may glimpse some evidence of God through our
behavior choices.) We literally get to the point here where
we make a choice on the basis of: "Lord, I'd like to do it
if it's good for You." If my action makes Him "look good"
to others, then the first two tests—my own good, and the
good of my neighbor—can't help being passed.

We have to be very careful that we don't simply tell
someone else what is good for him or her. What God
really wants for us is that we eventually come around to
choosing what is good, through the process of life—not
that somebody else tells us what is good or bad. If we
really want what God wants, circumstances will push us
toward the end of choosing the good. When we get into
something difficult or make a bad choice, that's what the

Scripture is for: to reprove us and help us work through it. Christ came for those who are having trouble. Trouble gives Him a chance to communicate with us. Trouble rips off a layer of insulation, a layer of apathy, a layer of culture that builds up around us; it exposes the edge of our sensitivity to the point that it begins to respond properly to what's good. It's in the context of "choosing a behavior" that I think sexuality can most helpfully be considered among young people: there are some things that are just not good choices for teenagers—or, may I add, for adults.

It always fascinates me that the two things that move high schoolers most at the Young Life camps are really one and the same. During the evening talks, without fail they are most absorbed by the talk on the Cross, God's expression of total love for His creatures. Next to that it is the talk on sexuality, our expression of love for each other, that causes them to respond. Both of these are efforts to explain love.

It is intellectually stimulating for some of them to talk about who Jesus is and the nature of man's inclination to sin; but that is not the real concern. When we get to the Cross there is total involvement; that is real. Then the last day I talk about sexuality from the standpoint of behavior; that's probably where kids are more than any place. "As a Christian how do I live?" they ask. "Give me a guideline." So I explain, "It's not possible to live the Christian life apart from the power of the Spirit. It's impossible! I fall on my face. But the Spirit of God wants to live it through me. That's why the Incarnation is so vital; it's God needing to live His life through us, God wanting to be felt in our behavior, seeking to come out of us in a visible display of love wherever we are."

One day this talk triggered a new insight in me: When God comes into our lives the beloved disciple, John, calls it the "new birth." Paul calls it the "new creation" (2 Cor. 5). It dawned on me: This human process of choosing is a continuing process of personal creation just as surely as God's expression of Creation in Nature is a continuing process. Our new life in Christ must go through similar steps; there is a development process that goes on in us too.

In *Until The Sun Dies,* Jastrow talks about the survival of the fittest, about a creature's developing through a survival mentality. In a sense that's barbaric to me; it's minimal in my thinking. What God is trying to perfect is the *highest* good; it's a pulling of all creation to the point where it brings glory to Him, because creation is *for* Him. In our personal lives mere survival cannot be our goal; we must continue to seek to produce the very *best* within us; and this is done by an unending sequence of decisions willfully to choose maturity rather than instant gratification.

It's a new humanity that God seeks—people who are changing, developing, becoming "more." All the potential we have is infused at the moment of spiritual conception, just as in the physical conceiving of a child; but we're given the privilege—throughout our lives—of participating in the choosing process, so that potential can be honed. You know what? The choosing process is a creation plan for people!

14. *The Loving Dimension*

The doorbell rang as Ruth and I were cleaning up the dinner dishes. It was later than usual; some of the boys had come by to see Bill and Randy, and we had been horsing around with them. I looked at Ruthie and asked, "You expecting company, sweetheart?" She giggled in that way I've learned to love and elbowed me back from the sink. "You'd better not keep him waiting out there. I thought the Prince of Wales might drop by tonight."

The doorbell sounded again as I threw the towel down and headed for the door. I switched on the light as I opened the door to find one of our more beautiful friends looking at me through a swollen eye which was rapidly turning black. Tears streaked her face; her mouth twisted in an effort to speak.

"What in the world happened, Elsie?" I blurted in total astonishment, reaching out to draw her inside. "Ruthie!"

After settling her on the couch with a cup of tea we heard the same story we have heard a number of times since. Elsie and Fred were both friends of ours. He was a professor at a nearby college; she was a gregarious

gamine spirit, a delight to all of us who knew her. This evening, and over the next few days, a less obvious side of their marriage began to unfold. Elsie had run away to our house to hide from her husband. He had physically beat her, and of course, this wasn't the first time she had been abused. She was shaken at every level, confidence gone. There was no way she could imagine returning to a man she loved, but one who turned on her in a passionate moment and mistreated her.

Ruthie bathed her wounds and applied the ice pack and the salve. Becky put clean sheets on her bed and turned back the covers for Elsie before bedding herself down in the family room. I threw another log on the fire, and we talked till it burned into ashes.

A couple of things have impressed me over the years about marriage, and about the ongoing effectiveness of marriage. The first part is the need to keep romantic love alive. And that takes work. And some of us will be more skilled at that than others. But the thing that comes out of that romantic love, it seems to me, is that we learn to *care* for each other. It's the caring about what's happening to each other's life that is the long-haul demonstration of love, the one we can live with over the years, the one that has longevity to it. The romantic love will come and go, but what it accomplishes is an atmosphere and a capacity to demonstrate more caring actions, and that caring is what we long for. Deep down we want somebody who really cares for us, in the little things, the everyday considerations of our lives.

The next morning I got a call from Fred. "Bill? Do you know where Elsie is? She always comes back before—"

"Yes, Fred, she's here at our house."

"Thank God!" he sighed. "I'll be right over."

"No, we don't want you to come here yet, Fred," I told him. "You and I will have to talk first." We set a time that afternoon to play a game of handball and have a talk over dinner.

"Well, how do you treat a woman, Bill?" he asked after he'd talked awhile about Elsie. "Could you write something down that I could read and follow?" I was shaking my head at him. Here was this brilliant teacher who was a clumsy lover. He did not understand the gentleness, the tenderness—the caring about what his wife would like. All of the expressions and forms of caring for a woman were unfamiliar to him. He had

never seen them in his boyhood home. He had not
known anybody or ever watched anybody who expressed
this kind of caring, so he could not figure out how to be a
caring person. He would make an overture of love to
Elsie, thinking that a woman ought to respond to
whatever he would do, because "Surely she ought to
know I want to love her!" When she didn't, or couldn't
respond to him, he would abuse her. I tried to explain to
him that what he wants to do to, or for, a woman is not
necessarily what will open her love for him.

"You can't take that for granted," I explained. "There has
to be a right time for loving, and a right place. The
circumstances are very important." We mentioned little
things that might prevent her from responding to his
love-making, even when she wished to: a resentment or
disappointment, sheer weariness, an expected phone call,
even the cars swishing past an open window. There are
ever so many other blocks. He wanted me to talk about
the actual moves he could make. What do you do first?
What you do second? It was as if an informational door
was opening for him and he was trying to grasp the
elements of how to care. We talked about how to change
from a selfish perspective to one of finding out how the
other person feels. Instead of thoughtlessly rushing his
wife, I suggested he stop and ask, "What is Elsie feeling?
What is she asking? What does she want?"

Over the years since, Fred and Elsie have gradually
learned how to care for each other, but at that point their
lack of communication was terrible! He didn't understand
how she felt at all. How they struggled as they learned to
be thoughtful of each other in all the many choices a day

brings! But how thrilling it has been for us to watch God's creative love released into their marriage.

People often do not understand how important thoughtfulness is in building each other's lives: that sensitivity to another's desires and needs opens up a widening capacity for love to respond; that the little touches in a marriage (or in a family) create a special climate where love can flourish. Ruth has been helpful to me in guiding me into an understanding of how to give my love to her. She has had to express—verbally—what she likes, what she dislikes, what she longs for, to enumerate these things in detail to me. That is part of loving. Talking is a way to get to know each other, a way of revealing more of who we are, so we can know better how to care. Ruthie's sharing reveals so much about a woman that is not a natural part of a man's understanding. It adds a breadth to our experience that makes the climate for loving so much more comfortable. It opens up many more alternatives to us in the giving and receiving of love.

To be able to grasp the idea that we are sexual beings who have far greater parameters than intercourse or orgasm frees up a loving dimension that affects all of life. The caressing, the holding, the unexpected kiss, the words of appreciation, the tender touch of a hand, the placing of an arm around a waist, the rubbing of a back, the passing of a wink or a special glance—all are signals of belonging, of caring, of communicating. They are ongoing reminders of our sexuality, and quite the spice of life. One little act of tenderness can make a whole day. It's marvelous to watch the response to that sort of thoughtfulness. If people could only understand that the broader expression of caring is what is being yearned for! If we could only see the sexual act as our highest expression of love, not our lowest! I see it as the crowning act of love, built up to through all the little expressions of caring that precede it and make it ever so appropriate and welcome.

God's crowning act here on the human scene was the coming of His Son. After He had given to the human race the exalted place in Creation, it had become a defeated, beaten, fallen crowd. Who in the world would figure that God would take the time and trouble to come into this crummy scene? But to complete the process of Creation through His Incarnation, the Son did enter the human race—to restore order, to bring in new life. To relate this to the marriage bond is obvious to me. Intercourse at its best brings new aliveness to a married couple, restoring communication and confidence.

Marriage, as I understand it, is to be started by a mutual commitment to care for each other's life. Then it's to be an adventure together: sexually, intellectually, vocationally, spiritually, every way. The sexual is part of the whole; it plays one role, not the whole cast. It's a coming together that's symbolic of what life with God is intended to be: "Just as you, Father, live in me and I live in you, I am asking that . . . they may be one, as [you and I] are one . . ." (John 17:21, Phillips). There's an intercourse that takes place in the physical world; we understand that. In the spirit world it is very much the same, even as the commitment is the same. It isn't that you *love* God so much to start with; it's that you make the

choice to commit yourself to God, and then you hang on!
It won't necessarily be all happiness, but it is a choice in
favor of commitment. I wonder if marriage ever was
intended to be all happiness: Happiness and fulfillment
are not the same. There is a fullness, a rightness, a
oneness that comes through commitment, a process
which requires the 'worse' as well as the 'better' to pull it
off. It probably never was intended to be a diet of pure
ecstasy. How would we ever know the peace and joy of
being comforted if it weren't in the context of also being
hurt or scared or upset?

Caring is part of the creative process God has built into
His world. It is part of the process of becoming,
developing, nurturing, maturing. Caring pulls out of
people more of what is already there. It's like the sun
coming out and the rain falling on the earth making it
more productive. Caring puts people at ease, makes them
comfortable in the sense of being at ease with themselves,
with each other, with the situation, so that those things
that we are naturally designed to produce in our lives can
rise to the surface and be revealed.

My brother told me about a pinched nerve he had down
his neck and arm. It makes his fingers go to sleep; he's
had terrible headaches. He goes for physical therapy to
alleviate the effects of the pinched nerve; and the
rubbing, the massaging, the applying of heat, the gentle
treatment of that part of the neck, that tender kind of
caring for his physical condition puts him at ease, and
turns off a lot of the negative energies. All of that tender
caring begins to produce health generally in my brother's
body. That kind of caring in a marriage produces the
health—in both partners—that releases them to be and to

function the way they are supposed to. Caring allows the creative process to continue or to be restored. When problems arise, they are usually most effectively met by someone providing care, whether it's personal care or medical care, legal, financial or technical care. It's a brand of caring that makes the difference.

How often have we heard some lonely person say, "I might have to go to the hospital again," and perhaps thought, "That's just what she wants to do." I can understand that. You can find a very caring experience in a hospital, especially if you're used to living alone. All those people are there to take care of you. They may be slow to answer your call button, but they are paid to be tuned in to where you hurt and to provide what will alleviate that hurt. They are hired to care, to pay attention to those patients who are their specific assignment.

God looked at His Creation and saw that it was good. And when man or woman has some trouble, it does not mean that they are not good; it means that they have a problem that needs to be taken care of, and it can be taken care of through the proper kind of caring. Associated with Creation in my mind is the knowledge that God created the person, and that we are to provide the healing for that creation process to continue properly in each other. Through our caring the original designs of God are freed up in those we love. If they are bound up to where they can no longer function, they can be oiled by the caring so that once again they can roll.

Two imperfect people come together to form an imperfect marriage. The two imperfects don't make a perfect any more than $0 + 0 = 1$. It seems to me that the way to comfort each other in marriage is to start out by saying that no marriage is perfect, but that the union is meant to contain a great deal of love. That immediately focuses on the right element: Our loving is never perfect, but it is a caring for our imperfection. Love is to make up for those gaps in us; caring fills in our holes. Love is for imperfect people because it supplies something that is missing. That's exactly where I see love entering into a marriage to make the husband and the wife worth more than they would be worth by themselves. Two imperfect people come together to apply the missing ingredients in each other, the necessary ingredients that can create an entirely new life. That to me is the loving dimension.

15. *Old Hat*

Some years ago I met an old man who gave me a simple
maxim that has profoundly affected the way I look at
people. It is so simple, your eyes will pass right over it
here on this page unless we mark it large in capital letters.
Let's do it:

> EVERY PERSON YOU EVER MEET
> KNOWS AT LEAST ONE THING
> YOU DON'T KNOW

In the years that have passed I've found that this
"seeking" posture with people gives all of life an air of
expectancy, of further discovery about to be made. It
brings brightness into a room full of people, spontaneity
into a marriage. It opens a larger world beyond my
restricted outlook.

How would it be if we took the same maxim and revised it
to read: *The person who is most familiar to you always has
something new waiting to emerge that you don't know about.*
Now, that could make you suspicious, if you insist on
being suspicious, or it could make you more caring than
you've ever been.

What makes a bride and groom lose the glow of their first
love? Why do we ever take those closest to us for granted?
How can the people we love most ever get to be "old
hat"? Is it partly because we stop "seeing" them? Is it that
familiarity which makes us comfortable with things as
they are, and prevents us from seeing each other in the
dazzling light of what we could be? Is there something of
fear in us that makes us threatened by looking for the
unfamiliar, the unknown, the strange in each other?
Where is the revealing to be made, if we cling only to
what we already know? How can I love my husband or
wife "more today than I did yesterday and less than I will
tomorrow" if I don't go beyond the limitations of the
familiar?

In the process of writing this book something has
happened to the feminine half of the team. After nearly
two decades of widowhood, and I might add successful,
productive, happy years they have been, Char has said
"yes" to a friend of the family and has gotten married
again. She was most concerned about having become a
different person over the years when they had been out
of touch, a person who would not be the same as the
friend expected or remembered. The truth is, of course,
that she is not a different person, but that there is a lot
more of her to be revealed—which, of course, he knew.
There is something dynamic going on here that embraces
the new, the strange, the unfamiliar, and in doing so,
creates more love to be expressed. Something is
happening in both persons that allows this to happen:
first, each person has become more in the intervening
years, and is able to see that; second, in each person a
perceiving is taking place about the other that looks for

more to be unfolded. These two parts of the process are complementary: that's the way relationships grow. Something is revealed by one, which opens up and enables the other to reveal more. Again it's part of the creation process going on in two people who are committed to love each other.

When a person becomes related to Christ and receives the limitless life of God, he or she becomes a new creation, and that newness then enables more creation to take place in another. The new revelation in one enhances the new revelation in the other, which means that in people and in their relationships there are limitless possibilities when God enters. When we stop to consider the ramifications of creation in a marriage, it's an absolute mind-blower. We begin to see there is no end to the new revelations of truth, the new creations taking place, the new unfolding of love. It gets so exciting always to expect a new facet to turn up. There's something of the Old Testament quality of welcoming "the stranger at your gate" in this way of viewing those in your home as "sent ones"—something of the "entertaining angels unawares" feel. We can learn to see in a spouse, or a family member, the potential that is there for a new person to emerge, a stranger to be revealed out of the familiar. If only we would allow some hospitable spirit to flow from us to care for that "stranger" emerging out of the familiar, to embrace that newness being born in the midst of the office humdrum or laundry routine that can so readily blot out the image! It cannot happen if we aren't looking for it, or don't expect it, or turn it away. There has to be a *wanting* to meet the stranger, a *looking* for the newness emerging. I have to be *believing* it will happen, or it won't.

Believing that it will be is the key. For if I am not
believing in the wonders which God has built into my
loved one, then I am believing in something quite the
opposite.

This is an enormous jump from where most of us live.
What allows us to make that jump? St. Paul's famous
chapter on love—1 Corinthians 13— lists some of the
very practical characteristics of love: full of endurance,
patience, kindness; not envious or jealous; not boastful,
haughty, or inflated with pride; not rude or self-seeking;
not touchy or resentful; doesn't keep track of wrongs or
rejoice at injustice, but rejoices in the right. Love bears
up under everything, believes the best of everyone, has
no end to its hope, and never becomes obsolete or comes
to an end.

I love to watch Richie's eyes gleam when he sees
something new. The wonder and enthusiasm that springs
naturally from a child helps pull the best out of people.
It's the "little boy" and "little girl" in us that gives us the
capacity to respond to life, to live it, and to love it. The
ability to see new things and react with delight allows
others to come alive again and to reveal the freshness
they thought was lost. It's not too far from what Christ
said about the Kingdom of God, "Except you become as a
little child you cannot enter the Kingdom of God." And
isn't the Kingdom of God about the best place to be?

16. *A Matter of Survival*

Years ago, during the war in the Pacific, I was assigned to a small naval aircraft carrier as a damage control officer. We were used to "qualifying" pilots who were learning to land on our tiny floating "postage stamp" strip out in the middle of the vast ocean. Flying those TBM and TBF-type planes was a tough job; they were heavy rascals, and when their engines were cut off they would land like rocks on the deck.

One clear summer day will never be fully erased from my mind. I was aft, along with the other men assigned to Damage Control Center. We were responsible to figure out the ballast for the ship and to give the orders needed to maintain the carrier for any kind of service. Minding our own business, about midafternoon, we were suddenly jolted off our feet by a torpedo blast which hit the ship forward below the water line between two watertight areas. Both were ripped open. We had been unaware of any enemy submarines in the area, but there was no doubt we had been severely damaged. Water, flooding in at a dangerous speed, started to pull the ship down toward the port bow. In order to save the carrier and the majority of the men aboard, the captain on the bridge gave the terse order to close the hatches. It was a terrible experience for those of us in the center to find out later that seventeen men on the other side of those watertight doors lost their lives.

On any kind of ship there is a critical point: up to that point you can take water and still float; beyond that point, if you continue to take water, the ship goes down. If you close the hatches you'll stop taking water; but there is no way you can move the people out of the danger area before those doors are closed.

And there is no other way to stop the powerful intake of water; you have to give up the damaged portion of the vessel, which means all the people who are in it, as well. It's a save-what-you-can-save sort of operation, and the harsh reality keeps you from talking in terms of whether it's right or wrong to close the doors. Is it ever right? Is it ever not wrong? You have to talk, instead, in terms of survival for the majority.

That's how I've come to look on some marriages that flounder and start to capsize. It's a matter of survival for the individuals involved, the last chance of a drowning person: "I've got to do something. I've got to get out or I can't make it."

How we have struggled to hold people together over the years! Fought to stay right in the middle, straddling the separation with both the husband and the wife! Hurt as we've watched them hurt in the strain of tearing apart! Tried to protect each of them from the utter loneliness and rejection of divorce. We've stood in that personal

gap—with friends—in Colorado, in Illinois, in Oregon, Washington, California. We have listened and counseled and prayed; welcomed, fed, and housed; and in the process we have been stretched, and our own marriage has been strained and strengthened. Our conclusions are not the same as they once were on the matter of divorce, but the question of whether or not to "close the hatches" is always a personal one. That decision can never be judged by the rest of us.

The more we see of these marital breakups, the less it seems they have to do with right and wrong. You can't speak simply of a moral lapse; rather, the breakup stems from a failure of the love relationship to carry the load. It's demanding too much for the bridgework between two lives to bear. For whatever reason, there is a weakening; maybe the partners don't understand enough of life to build enough of a foundation. They are not aware of the toll that stress or strain will take. The engineers used the wrong materials. There was a hasty decision, premature, uninformed. Who understands completely? Who can look back and say, "He was to blame." Or, "She was at fault."

If the bridge can't carry the load, I sense it has to do with the *breaking point of persons*—with their health, with their capacity to see clearly, to listen well, to care enough, to feel the other's point of pain, to desire the other's good, or with an inability to let God be God in their lives. When the bridge of communication begins to crack or crumble, then the bridge of love is soon to follow.

Communication—significant communication—is the process of revealing, opening up. Walling yourself apart so you can't be seen, so you can't be known, refusing to reveal yourself creates a blockade—fear, distrust, misunderstanding—a weakness; and gradually the bridge of love comes tumbling down.

I'm captivated by this idea of revelation. As we've observed in an earlier chapter, Creation is an act of God to reveal Himself. Then the completion of the revelation process is the Incarnation. Christ comes in the flesh, God's human form lives among us and *speaks* to us about the things of God. Christ talks about them, as well as demonstrating them. Creation is a demonstration; Christ's life is a demonstration. But . . . Christ puts words to His behavior too; and it is audacious of us to think that life by itself says it all. We must not expect that the way we live can communicate without our articulating what we think, feel, want. I'm convinced that we have to have words for each other; our conduct is not clear enough. For instance, I was thinking of how essential it is to say "I love you." It's essential to ask forgiveness. Ruth and I just went through that again; she felt I had really crushed her in the presence of some very dear friends. It really hurt her, and I thought that if I wanted to go back and heal that hurt there was no way but to say, "I really am sorry. I apologize. I wouldn't hurt you knowingly for anything."

Unless the revealing has a substance to it, however, if it is not of the "creation essence," it won't be solid enough to get your weight out on it. You must sense that the articulation is solid, genuine, and real. In Creation God says, "You can know Me by perceiving what's taking place." That's the quality we need in revealing ourselves to each other. If there isn't that quality through which I can know my husband or wife in that deeper sense, then I probably don't really want to be known. Communication breaks down when there is nothing significant being shared, nothing really going on beyond the facts of the day.

Ruthie and I have an arrangement to sit down and talk before the dinner hour. This is equaling discovery in our lives together, and we both are eager to keep that date each day. It's more than talking. It's opening up. It's stepping into the risky places of our lives, places where we know we may have been hurt and therefore have a tendency to protect rather than reveal. But in the revealing there is a flow of love. It is a very simple thing, a commitment to a time and to a process we believe can

happen between us. It's a top priority, to secure the
bridge of love.

But what if one person can't go beyond a certain point?
What if a gross imbalance tips the marriage toward the
port bow? Is there the possibility it's damaged to the point
of closing the hatches? Is it possible that "the mix" is
wrong? Do I lean on the marriage commitment anyway?
Is it a duty that prevails even when there isn't the capacity
in one party to move on? Are we committed to a slow
death?

We all know people whose marriage was miserable, or at
best mediocre, in the early years; but upon sticking it out,
perhaps through the child-raising years, they have
discovered a whole new life together, after twenty, thirty,
forty years of marriage. It's exciting to watch this happen.

Stages of life are very real, and time *is* a factor. There
was little in common in the early years, except for the
children, in one couple we know well. But anticipating
retirement has become a happy expenditure of joint ideas
and energies in an entirely new setting which requires
new learning and working toward new goals. Now, after
more than thirty years of marriage, they are thriving. But
their children are all divorced. Did the children's failure
in marriage make them more determined to succeed in
theirs? Or did their failure to make their early marriage
years full of love influence their children's desire to "close
the hatches" and get out? To tell a couple of despairing
young marrieds, "Hang in there! It'll be all right in
another 30 years" confronts them with a long haul. God's
kind of love is willing to commit itself till death. There *is*
a time factor. Real love does require commitment to allow

love to develop. There is something to "hanging in there," believing that it will be so good that it's worth the long haul. But . . .

It reminds me of the old days when I used to run the mile. The first lap would be so exhilarating. The second became a bit boring. The third was utterly miserable; and the fourth very satisfying. Someone has broken the process of married love into five distinct stages: (1) the dream, (2) the disillusionment, (3) the despair, (4) a new awakening, and (5) mature love. Paul's description of love in 1 Corinthians—"believing, enduring, hoping"—is the duty side of love, but it's a love that means it can happen! And it's worth working for:

> Love knows no limit to its endurance, no end to its trust, no fading of its hope; it can outlast anything. It is, in fact, the one thing that still stands when all else has fallen (1 Cor. 13:7, Phillips).

There is an alternate way that may be second-best, but necessary in certain cases. That is to say, "The mix is wrong. It can't work. It's ruining us both. I can't stand it. I've got to get out." That course is apparently the quicker one. But if you bail out, you're delaying—or detouring—the process. You're breaking the chain of creative loving you began together. You "go back to Go" and start over again. In some cases, I've had to admit this may be the only way to survive, for God's ideal, in fact, is always balanced against our human limitations. The fact that we have limits does not turn off God's love, but it may very well mean that we will damage ourselves, or someone else, as we dash headlong against His universal principles for relationships.

"I still believe divorce is sin," a fifty-year-old man told me as the settlement with his wife of twenty-five years drew to a close. "But in the midst of the anger, the grief and loneliness, the pain, I'm finding that God is meeting us even in our sin."

Sin is a fact in our world, and it does cause pain. When marriage fails, less than the desire of God has been fulfilled. Tearing apart the close grafting of human lives is a grave disruption of His pure desire.

When the Pharisees tested Jesus regarding divorce, He answered,

> "Haven't you read that the One who created them from the beginning made them male and female and said: 'For this cause shall a man leave his father and mother, and shall cleave to his wife; and the twain shall become one flesh?' So they are no longer two separate people, but one. No man therefore must separate what God has joined together."
> "Then why," they retorted, "did Moses command us to give a written divorce-notice and dismiss the woman?"
> (Matthew 19:4-7, Phillips)

It is helpful to look at the different translations of Jesus' answer in Matthew 19:8. The King James is the most familiar: "because of the hardness of your hearts," and the Living Bible is similar, "in recognition of your hard and evil hearts." Good News for Modern Man says, "because you are so hard to teach," and The New English Bible takes the same line with "because you were so unteachable." J. B. Phillips gives us "because you knew so little of the meaning of love," and Clarence Jordan, in his modern Cotton Patch Version with a southern accent,

gives us, "Moses let you divorce your wives because of
your own bullheadedness. But it was not that way to start
with."

A young man has reentered our lives after thirteen years
of education, marriage, child-rearing, and divorce. He
was a high school kid in one of our Young Life clubs at
the turn of the sixties. What happened to him he
describes as an unconscious withdrawal from all that was
meaningful, before he awakened to the reality that he was
in a mental hospital, depressed, away from his God, his
wife, his family. He tried to pick up the pieces of his life
and go on. He lost the presence of Christ; but he knew
that was his problem, not Christ's. The realization that
Christ has always been there—from that high school club
and on through the lostness and the pain—overwhelms
him, and this is what helps him pull meaning back into
life now. The fact that Christ never left him allows him to
go on with the hurt, the new people and experiences, his
own feeling of "I caused it." Whatever blame or fault
there was, he assumes it, and I appreciate that, but I
know that he and his wife are both victims.

It's so difficult for people to communicate the wreckage
left by divorce. I mean, you can't point to the damage;
you can't see the wreck as you can in an accident or a
death, but we ought to treat it that way. As I listen to
people who are being crushed by the debris of their
marriage I see the terrific responsibility that is ours, as
people of God, not to judge them in any way, or to feel
they are less than we are. We need to support them as we
would support anyone after a tragedy, when a
frightened, bewildered lostness, confusedness comes over

a shock victim. They need to be handled gently, tenderly, carefully, patiently. Less and less should we be sitting around in the rightness or wrongness of the divorce; we need to try to work toward the recovery of an individual, the restoration of a life!

In the parable of the prodigal son there are two cases: the son who obviously is having struggles to make life work for him, and the other son who is not at all obvious, but is struggling silently. I didn't used to see the hurt, the struggle, in the marriage partner who took the aggressive action for divorce. I only saw him or her as someone who had found someone or something he or she liked better, and who was cutting out; but I've come to believe that the shock is just as great there as it is in the person who is left. The private debate going on within—whether staying or leaving offers the best chance for a mature life, often for both spouses—creates intense turmoil and confusion. There is a tremendous amount of fear and pain in the person who first sees the hole in the sinking ship. The more aggressive action usually will do a better job of camouflaging that person's pain, while the other spouse is visibly suffering; but grief, numbness, disappointment, anger, can haunt the aggressor, too.

Christ's statement to the Pharisees, "You knew so little of the meaning of love," comes back to me again and again as I watch the bridge of love crumble. Why, why, why? I hear all around me. Perhaps faith is not strong enough, the love of God not clear enough. Perhaps the attitudes are not caring enough, or the emotions too childish to bear the weight of a relationship that started out so ecstatically. " 'London Bridge is falling down,' and it could be I'll get my life crushed unless I get away from the debris as it falls all around me." Isn't it like the watertight hatches on the sinking ship? Save what you can. You can talk about the rightness or wrongness of a divorce, but when a person is going down for the third time, that is futile. It doesn't fit. Is it ever right? Is it ever not wrong?

We cannot judge. It is far bigger than that. When you are so pulled apart, so used up that you cease to be the reflection of God that you once were, is there virtue in merely hanging on? Which is the greater of the two evils—to lose the "me" in the attempt to save the "other," or to rescue the "me"? Isn't it a matter of survival for at least two lives?

17. Friends: Beyond Sexuality

Between the rearing of our first children and the rearing of our last one, I see such a difference. Ruth and I are old enough to be Richie's grandparents, and it gives us such a different feeling. I feel I can be his friend without manipulating him to my goals. I was not able to do that with our first three children because I was trying too hard to be a good father. I'm not trying to be a "good father," per se, to Richie; what I am doing is offering myself to the little guy. It's a beautifully relaxed thing. I'm not looking for any return; but I'm getting an overwhelming response!

The other evening I was deeply moved, and the tears were rolling quietly down my cheeks. Richie, noticing, climbed up in my lap and said, "I hardly ever get to see you cry, Dad." Together we talked about the meaning of tears and we shared the goodness of being able to feel deeply.

In our society I see little room for people to have as their objective the simple pleasure of being with a person in order to be a friend. I have come to a sharp realization that friendship is not essential to the accomplishment of

the goals in most people's lives; thus, friendship is a very rare kind of love. It is not coaxed, paid off, shoved, dragged, enticed in a hundred ways, to do the work at hand.

To me, friendship is the most costly love, because it is all expenditure. There is no return to be expected. If there is a return, that is a bonus. Friendship asks and expects no payment. It doesn't fit into the categories that we understand, such as doing something out of obedience. A child obeying his parents may occasionally be acting out of love; but the obedience is more often motivated by a desire to please the parents, to get along in the family, to make things run relatively smoothly. The act of obeying usually tries to accomplish some end. It's when we're not trying to get anything done, that we can have a friendship kind of love.

Even in marriage friendship can be skipped; it is not an essential in our day. The *eros* kind of love is certainly present, and the concept of commitment can be fully regarded in a marriage where there is no true friendship. In the lives of most people, friendship comes way down the line. To take the time to build a friendship for the sake of sharing deeply is indeed rare, and the friendship level of love is a very deep level.

C. S. Lewis has written so eloquently in *The Four Loves* about friendship: ". . . the least *natural* of loves; the least instinctive, organic, biological, gregarious and necessary. It has least commerce with our nerves; there is nothing throaty about it; nothing that quickens the pulse or turns you red and pale. It is essentially between individuals; the moment two men are friends they have in some degree drawn apart together from the herd. Without Eros none of us would have been begotten and without Affection none of us would have been reared, but we can live and breed without Friendship. The species, biologically considered, has no need of it."*

Friendship is strangely separate from the material affairs of life. We will go out to dinner with companions or acquaintances, and have a great time; but meeting the everyday needs of life is basically an interruption, a distraction of the always-too-short time friends have together. "Let him be to me a spirit," Emerson states in his essay on Friendship. "A message, a thought, a

---

*C. S. Lewis, *The Four Loves* (New York: Harcourt, Brace & Co., 1960), p. 88.

sincerity, a glance from him I want, but not news, nor pottage."*

Companionship is often the matrix out of which friendship is born. It goes on in locker rooms, pubs, country clubs, mess halls, boats, parks, kitchens, backyards. Activities such as hunting, fishing, sewing, lunching, playing cards are often referred to in terms of friendship, but these "friends" are more often "companions." This is not to disparage companions; rather, it is to distinguish between the two.

Lewis explains that "Friendship arises out of mere Companionship when two or more of the companions discover that they have in common some insight or interest or even taste which the others do not share and which, till that moment, each believed to be his own unique treasure (or burden). . . . It is when two such persons discover one another, when . . . with immense difficulties . . . or . . . amazing . . . speed, they share their vision, it is then that Friendship is born. And instantly they stand together in an immense solitude. . . . The very condition of having Friends is that we should want something else besides Friends. Where the truthful answer to the question, *Do you see the same truth?* would be, 'I see nothing and I don't care about the truth; I only want a Friend,' no Friendship can arise—though Affection, of course, may. There would be nothing for the Friendship to be *about;* and Friendship must be about

---

*Emerson, *Essays* (New York: Clark, Given, and Hooper) University edition, p. 131.

something, even if it were only an enthusiasm for dominoes or white mice. Those who have nothing can share nothing; those who are going nowhere can have no fellow travelers."*

It strikes me how infinitely more we have to be about than dominoes! Being friends is different to me than following God's command to love each other. The *agape* kind of love is an act of obedience to please the Father rather than a case of mutual interests drawing two people together. You cannot command somebody to be a friend. Emerson says, "We talk of choosing our friends, but

*C. S. Lewis, *The Four Loves,* pp. 96, 97, 98.

friends are self-elected. Reverence is a great part of it."
Friendship comes as the result of seeing that the essence
of life is in giving when there is no end to be
accomplished—when you have no right to any claim on
anything other than that you both happen to belong to
God.

That truth stands out to me as I read the letter Paul
wrote to the Christians in Thessalonica: "You know what
manner of men we were among you for your sake" (1
Thess., 1:5 KJV). He quite forgets the end result in the
intensity of primary living. Paul's purpose was not to get
people to do anything; he was a man with a rare truth
who lived with them openly for their sake. Then if the
Holy Spirit moved his friends to hear the words that
would expound the truth of the Gospel, then those words
would be spoken. In Paul's case his friends did listen; but
that was not why Paul became their friend. Because he
was gripped by the truth and tenderness of Jesus Christ,
his life was destined to be spent in intense pursuit of all
that life was meant to be. A life that spilled over in
enthusiasm ("Do you see the same truth?" or "Do you
care about the same truth?") would have had great appeal
to the truth-seekers in Paul's day. Being joint seekers of
the same truth, the same beauty, the same God, offers a
blazing and compelling attraction whenever we are
willing to live among people for their sake.

This kind of love that is neither pushing nor grasping is
unbelievable in our world. It is a love of mutuality, or
equality, in which you are neither masculine or feminine.
It goes beyond sexuality, beyond nationality, beyond role
or profession. It is being God's human creation, willing to

risk being human. Unembarrassed by material advantage or disadvantage, two human beings come together in a simple common search, on a common journey.

It looks to me as though God meant for love to be lived out on a unique basis of equality; He made man in His own image. Then when He walked in the cool of the Garden of Eden, He looked for His friends, and found them hiding from Him. His plan for equality was short-lived; and from Genesis 3 to Acts 2 this quality is missing in the biblical record. What God intended in Creation was to be revealed in the new humanity. What happened on the day of Pentecost brought the disciples into a celebrative, joyous relationship that broke language barriers and introduced a rare communion of love such as human beings had not known since Eden.

The entire panoply of God's Creation formed the vast platform for His kingdom to open, and those of us who are drawn to Him become that Kingdom. The population of the Kingdom is created by our response to the King, don't you agree? Being a friend, as I see it, is what we're about in the Kingdom. I'd like to suggest that while we see the birth of Jesus Christ ranking at the top of all human history, we do not want to limit ourselves to *talking* about the theology of Incarnation, except as it forms a model for us. Rather, we consider it methodology for those who make up the Kingdom. The deeper we go into our own hearts, the more likely we are to get a vital response from others. The response is overwhelmingly good when they can read vibrations that say, "Here is somebody who isn't after a thing. He doesn't want me to do anything, to give up anything. He is just offering himself unconditionally."

Like Martin Luther, I believe that as a friendship ripens, there will be a natural sharing in words of our very best understanding of the Gospel. It is an integral part of friendship to share the deepest of all personal things. Once we have reached this level with someone, we want certain things understood that we would not care at all to share with others. The Gospel to me is not something to throw around, or to exhibit in an impersonal fashion on a billboard. It's like when God told Moses, "You're on holy ground. Get your shoes off." That's the way I feel about the Gospel. When we get down to that level of sharing with a person, we are on holy ground.

It is audacious for us to think that any human experience by itself is sufficient to convey the immense good news of the Gospel. We have to put words to it eventually, even though in doing so we stumble. The Holy Spirit of God graciously takes that truth and uses everything He has going for Him; so the Truth we speak is better understood if we have taken even the earliest steps toward friendship.

While sharing a discovery can add new dimensions to the friendship, it can also drive a wedge between two people. Expressing innermost thoughts is always a risk. Friendship may be jeopardized, but you don't throw out the friend because something happens that you can't understand. You work it out on the basis that there is now more to explore. You're in a larger place than you were before this disruption.

This, to me, is why friendship is a vital aspect of propogation of the gospel. If, indeed, something does alienate or separate or hurt, friendship is the force that makes two individuals willing to go back and pick up the hurt and look at it together. What did happen? What are we finding out? If offense takes place without friendship who cares? Who will bother to want to repair the damage?

The Gospel I understand is given life in the Incarnation. If we think we can dispense with this, giving words only to those around us, then it seems to me we have not grasped the Gospel at all. The Gospel steps forth in the Incarnation, and in the human involvement of friendship we begin to call forth a new being in each other.

There are such thrilling examples of revolutionary change in the story of Christ and Zacchaeus. The whole story fascinates me:

> Then he went into Jericho and was making his way through it. And here we find a wealthy man called Zacchaeus, a chief collector of taxes, wanting to see what sort of person Jesus was. But the crowd prevented him from doing so, for he was very short. So he ran ahead and climbed up into a sycamore tree to get a view of Jesus as he was heading that way. When Jesus reached the spot, he looked up and said to him,
> "Zacchaeus, hurry up and come down. I must be your guest today."
> So Zacchaeus hurriedly climbed down and gladly welcomed him. [The RSV says, "joyfully received Him."] But the bystanders muttered their disapproval, saying, "Now he has gone to stay with a real sinner."
> But Zacchaeus himself stopped and said to the Lord, "Look, sir, I will give half my property to the poor. And if I have swindled anybody out of anything I will pay him back four times as much."
> Jesus said to him,
> "Salvation has come to this house today! Zacchaeus is a

descendant of Abraham and it was the lost that the Son of Man came to seek—and to save."

Luke 19:1-10, Phillips

They say there were two main routes through Jericho at this time, so Jesus had to choose one of them, and Zacchaeus had to be pretty sharp to anticipate which one of these routes Jesus and the parade would take. Being the chief collector of taxes, Zacchaeus was probably well known throughout the town. He wanted very much to see what sort of person Jesus was, "But the crowd prevented him from doing so." (This is the part the crowd usually plays.) The text tells us that Zacchaeus *ran* and climbed up into a tree. He must have had that very tree in mind; he must have known the area and remembered that specific branch hanging out over the road where he could sit. So perching himself up in the tree—very comfy—he watched Jesus come toward him. Suddenly Jesus stopped right underneath the branch, which probably shocked the bejabbers out of Zacchaeus. And he heard Jesus saying to him, "Zacchaeus, come down. I must be your guest today."

The first thing that is astonishing in this record is that Jesus called Zacchaeus by name. Where in the world did He find out his name? Did He get it when He walked into town and saw the big house on the edge of the city with the swimming pool, wondering what wealthy man lived there? Was he able to overhear talk about Zacchaeus as He walked through the town? Maybe He asked somebody, "Who is that fellow up in the tree?" I have always wondered how Jesus did know his name, because I am convinced that He did not pull that very personal bit of data out of His divinity. There was no "Hey, you up there—" Jesus recognized that a name is the most meaningful part of our human identity, the very first identifying feature we have. And that's how He approached Zacchaeus. He used his name.

It is always amazing to me that there are people who can go through life thinking that they don't have to really work on learning people's names, that it's not really important. "I can always remember faces but I have such a hard time remembering names," they say. As far as I can determine the matter is one of understanding how important names are, coupled with a willingness to work on remembering them. Some people take the trouble, others don't. If you are at all interested, you can do it by getting yourself into the framework of thinking about it. Usually when we meet someone new we are absorbed with how we are coming across and what we can say that will make an impression, rather than listening carefully to the other person and concentrating on catching the name. That's why it really thrills me that Jesus called Zacchaeus by name.

The other thing that is so remarkable to me is that out of the whole crowd, out of Jesus' entire march across Jericho, there was only one person He talked to in that town. He didn't talk to the mayor, or look up the owner of the Jericho Jewelry Store or the president of the Chamber of Commerce. He picked the little tax collector. Jesus wasn't there for a big speaking engagement, a prayer breakfast, an evangelistic campaign, or a TV appearance; He only addressed one person. He said to Zacchaeus, "I must be your guest." We are told that Zacchaeus hurriedly climbed down and gladly welcomed

Him—"joyfully received Him"—which makes me think of the passage in John's gospel:

> "He came unto His own and His own received Him not. But as many as received Him to them gave He power to become the sons of God, even to them that believe on His name" (John 1:11–12, KJV).

In the "receiving" of Jesus there is salvation, and Zacchaeus "received Him joyfully." The bystanders disapproved, "Now He has gone to be with a *real* sinner." Evidently they had two kinds of sinners in their scheme of things: sinners and real sinners. Of course, everything that happened is not recorded in the scripture, but before they even took off on the walk to his home, Zacchaeus stopped and said, "Look, Sir, I will give half of my property to the poor. If I have swindled anybody out of anything, I will pay them back four times as much."

Jesus had not said anything to Zacchaeus before this, as far as we know. We don't know what Zacchaeus thought he would see when he set out that day to find out what kind of a person Jesus was. He certainly did not have any premeditated hope of having a private conversation with Him! Yet the moment he got with Him he started to do something drastic! He was going to give half of his property to the poor. And *if* he swindled anything out of anybody . . . as if he didn't know! Zacchaeus knew he had swindled some people, so he said, "I'll pay him back four times as much."

It is overwhelming to me that just being in the presence of Jesus, this man started giving away the very thing that he had probably spent his entire lifetime trying to accumulate. Money was the dearest thing to this tax collector's heart. And now he wanted to give at least half of it to the poor! And he probably ended up giving a whole lot more away than he ever dreamed because he was going to give away four times what he swindled, too.

One of the amazing things to me was Zacchaeus' use of language in responding to God. Were these words of Zacchaeus "words of salvation"? Would we consider them appropriate words to indicate that some friend of ours had met Christ? Would we be able to say in response to words such as these, "Salvation has come to your house today," as the Lord did?

These words got me to thinking about what God did when He wanted to speak to us. First He spoke in Creation. When He wanted to speak a second time it was in Incarnation. It was after these first two primary expressions of God's love and concern that the written word came. His primary means of expressing the fact that He loves us dearly was nonverbal: one in the material universe, the other in human form. Only after these two acts did words come. It's the state of the heart, of course, that is important to the Lord. Words are important in that they can tell us something about where a person's heart is. In Zacchaeus' case, the words were, "I am going to give half of what I own to the poor." What I hear him saying is this, "What was Number One in my life is no longer number one. After meeting You, Lord, all that I have spent my whole life for is second place. You are up at the top now." And the thrilling thing is that Jesus answered him saying, "Salvation has come to this house

today. This is indeed a son of Abraham. This is the son of
faith. That was an act of saving faith."

I believe that salvation is connected with the way that
Zacchaeus received the Lord, when he got out of that tree
and *joyfully* received Him. That to me is the key to the
whole story. His words were an evidence to Christ that
Zacchaeus had decided to go in an entirely new direction.
It was a response of faith—getting out of that tree instead
of sitting up there saying, "Look, I don't know you, and
frankly I don't want you to meddle with my life. I just
wanted to see you." The fact that he hurried out of that
tree and joyfully received Jesus is the key to his salvation.
It was the leap he took without hesitation, as though all
his life he had been waiting for this moment of
encounter.

God could have spread the word about His love by
dropping leaflets on the world, but He didn't. He took
the time and trouble to become a human baby and come
to us personally. He spent a period of years in an attempt
to express to His friends what was in His heart.
Because we, too, are tied to space/time concepts, I believe
God expects us also to exercise this nonessential kind of
love in living out His life in our society today. The one
vehicle, humanly speaking, that gives us some chance of
success at this is friendship. Floodgates that are normally
closed swing open to reveal an inner truth, an inner
tenderness, a startling kind of caring.

In his play *The Burnt Flower Bed,* Ugo Betti expresses this
truth: "Nothing else matters half so much. To reassure

one another. To answer each other. Perhaps only *you*
can listen to me and not laugh. Everyone has inside
himself . . . what shall I call it? A piece of good news!
Everyone is . . . a very great, very important character! . . .
Every man must be persuaded—even if he is in rags—that
he's immensely, immensely important! Everyone must
respect him; and make him respect himself too. They
must listen to him attentively. Don't stand on top of him,
don't stand in his light. . . . Give him great, great hopes,
he needs them . . . especially if he's young."*

*Giovanni, act 2, p. 151, *Three Plays* by Ugo Betti (New York: Grove
Press, 1958).

18. A Rare Breed

A conversation between dear friends, clothed as it is in the fullness of personality, has a great deal to lose in translation onto the flat and solitary pages of a book. The raised eyebrow, shift in posture, unleashed guffaw, tears cresting into an extended pause, cannot be discounted as significant aids to a clearer understanding of what the words are trying to say. The human presence in its totality is a powerful vehicle of communication.

Considering this fact, we are aware that some of the insights we are attempting to share will be diluted or distorted on these isolated pages, whereas, in each other's presence any misrepresentations could have been pursued as they arose, and quite likely reshaped to mutual understanding and benefit. Some of what we have defined as Love here may perhaps be misconstrued as looseness. That's not what we believe Love is. Some of what we have welcomed as discovery of Truth will be put down as incomplete, or possibly even destructive. That's not what we believe Truth is either.

To blend Truth and Love in a way that will speed us toward increased clarity about each other, and about the purpose of life itself, appears to be a paramount goal in our human relations. We are somehow to work toward a synthesis of these two in our human behavior.

A dilemma develops over the two words Truth and Love as used in Scripture. Our human tendency is either to dote on Truth, which makes us so rigid we appear unloving and unapproachable; or to dote on Love, which makes us so flexible and accepting that we drift from one indulgent action to another with not enough regard for Truth. The fascinating reality is that God combines these two in Christ. In Him we see Truth and Love coincide. They meet and blend perfectly in the Incarnation. That is why an ardent person like Simon the zealot can sit down at the table of Christ with an exacting man like Matthew the tax collector. It is in Christ that these human disparities—Love and Truth—can come together. At the same time they bring "color" to the Body of Christ. These two poles, which in our humanity oppose one another, He can unify into one process. He does it so graciously, in such a way that neither is sacrificed. Take the example of the woman taken in adultery. When the Pharisees wanted to stone her so the law could be fulfilled, He said to them, "Let the one who is without sin cast the first stone." To the woman He said, "Go and sin no more." He was fully aware that these lawmongers had themselves broken the law and needed to learn compassion. He also knew that the best thing for the woman was to go from the scene of her abused love and live a new quality of life within the wholesome support of the law.

Always in the life of Christ we see love and truth blended beautifully; but when I look at our impact as Christians on the world we inhabit, it seems we more often pull the two apart. We get trapped in legalism, or we get trapped in permissiveness. I listened to a friend blowing off steam about doing business with these "blankety-blank

Christians." He had purchased a piece of equipment which was so large that in order to truck it to his plant he was forced to remove the motor and carry it separately. When he asked the manufacturer (the Christian) to sign the warranty, his request was refused. The manufacturer pointed out that the warranty read: If anything is taken off the machine the warranty is cancelled. The warranty, technically, was no longer valid, even though removing the motor in no way damaged the function of the purchased machine. So the exacter of the truth said, "I cannot sign the warranty." Love (grace) would have said, "I will sign it," at the same time pointing out to the purchaser—for his own protection—what the warranty stated.

My nature is antagonized by those who are only willing to be right. Rightness is not enough for human experience. It shuts down the process of Creation. There is more than rightness in the Incarnation. God expresses Truth in the crucifixion, the Truth being that God does demand payment for sin; but God also expresses Love in providing that payment. The very nature of God is winsome. All through Christ's time on Earth we find such a drawing power in His presence. We've talked about Zacchaeus, the woman in Simon's house, the leper, and there are untold others who experienced that quality and were healed by it. When the Truth of God is bathed in the Love of God, it has enormous drawing power.

Remember the eighth chapter of Matthew, when the leper comes to Christ? The law is broken twice. First, the leper breaks the law by coming as an "unclean" person into the presence of a clean one. Then Christ breaks the

law by reaching out and touching the untouchable. But
wait. What does the Savior do afterwards? He says, "Now
go and show yourself to the priest." After He has
exceeded the limits of the law He brings the man back
into the system of his day. He doesn't disregard the
system; what He does is go beyond it. He fulfills it far
beyond what the system thought it could hold.

When Truth touches a person in an expression that
comes out of Love, healing takes place. The forces of
re-creation are unleashed. Truth plus Love is bigger than
the system that says the leper can't be touched. That
remarkable blend overflows the system; it must be
allowed to flow through the restrictions, so it can
touch—the disease, the heartache, the rejection, the sin.
And the touch emanates kindness and goodness, but also
healing.

As had happened so many times in the course of our
conversations we were fumbling with something we
couldn't let go of. Old truths were rearranging
themselves with fresh meaning. We picked up first one
piece, then another:

> —Truth is meant to be kind. Love reaches out; Love is
> the expression of Truth that cannot be contained.
> —The system thought it had defined truth when it said
> that the leper was untouchable, but Truth was bigger
> than the system.
> —Truth is that disease is to be defeated. Disease is
> wrong; it's an encroachment against life.
> —Life is meant to be whole. Sin is an encroachment on
> that wholeness. Sin takes away from life.
> —Truth cannot abide anything that subtracts from

wholeness. Therefore, sin is an untruth encroaching upon life.

—Truth, in doing battle with untruth, heals. But healing comes through the vehicle of Love, through expressions of caring that may have to go beyond the boundaries set by the system.

Remember Pilate's question, "What is Truth?" The Truth is that God loves. The Truth is that God cares about people. And when the Truth of God's caring about people is expressed, we can look for it to go beyond that which any system can contain.

In a physical form we first see this expression in the Incarnation; but we are also to view these same attributes in one another. Paul talks to the Ephesians about a "new humanity." He describes them as a "new race of people." They are no longer simply Jew or Gentile; they are fused together into a new person, above and beyond either category.

We looked at each other in astonishment. "I'll bet that's why he's talking about a 'new race of people,'" I exclaimed. "Why didn't I ever think of that before?"

As natural men and women, we can only express one of these qualities at a time. We go for Love or we go for Truth. Only in a *new* race of people could both of these attributes be endemic. It's part of the new birth. When we're born into newness, a new race of people with God's life flowing in us, we can begin to blend attributes that were unblendable before. In the Incarnation God brought them together; now, He seeks a race of people who will continue to blend the attributes of divinity—a kingdom to demonstrate that God is Truth and God is Love. When you and I are born into this new humanity, we take into ourselves, very literally, a new quality of life that is God's and the blending of His Truth and Love, which begins to permeate our attitudes and acts, bringing healing and wholeness.

As we go about our daily lives, we are to be small samples of that blend. The magnetism of Christ is to be felt through us (as His tiny "magnets"), because as Christ's life comes into us, it wants to be released very practically in a gracious demonstration of the Truth. This is the ideal God seeks for in our relations with one another—in our marriages, our families, our friendships, our business dealings. And He seeks it also in our concern for the world and its crowded billions. This is the goal toward which we move, most of us ever so ploddingly throughout the days of our years, as we allow Christ to increase in us.

We are a rare breed, aren't we? I'm feeling condemned by my own words. How do I put into action these very things we are speaking about? A combination of kindness and firmness. Christ was the first member of this new humanity to express in action the blending of these two attributes which can only belong to divinity: Truth and Love. Yet these are to be the distinguishing marks of any offspring, any descendants of this "new race." As members of the new humanity we lose our identity as Jew or Greek, as Norwegian or African. Uniqueness no longer comes from skin color, type of hair, set of eyes, or cheekbones. It does not come from status or position. Our uniqueness comes through the blending of Love and Truth in the creative construction of the Kingdom. That blend is the trademark of the new breed.